MODERN SEX

MODERN SEX

LIBERATION AND ITS DISCONTENTS

EDITED WITH AN INTRODUCTION BY

MYRON MAGNET

IVAN R. DEE
CHICAGO 2001

With the exception of the Introduction, the contents of this book appeared originally in *City Journal*, published by The Manhattan Institute.

Library of Congress Cataloging-in-Publication Data:
   Modern sex : liberation and its discontents / edited with an introduction by Myron Magnet.
       p. cm.
   Previously published in City journal.
   Includes index.
   ISBN 1-56663-383-4 (cloth : alk. paper) — ISBN 1-56663-384-2 (pbk. : alk. paper)
   1. Man-woman relationships. 2. Sex. 3. Love. I. Magnet, Myron.
HQ801 .M63 2001
306.7—dc21   2001028999

CONTENTS

INTRODUCTION

The sexual revolution has failed in its own terms. It promised to make us all happier, freer, more fulfilled, more alive. Now, almost four decades later, with the Summer of Love and the years of swinging behind us, with our attitudes and our behavior unrecognizably transformed, with our culture so changed that the *New York Times* asks us seriously to consider whether the unsimulated sex scenes in recent mainstream movies constitute art rather than the hard-core pornography from which they are indistinguishable, where's the happiness?

Yes, there is much more voluptuous rubbing together of two intestines, as Diderot unglamorously put it two centuries ago—so much so that it seems indefatigable, almost nonstop. Our advertising, entertainments, literature, and conversation all celebrate sex of every description and at almost all ages, and our health-club workouts keep us in fighting trim for it. Our universities put on sex fairs, complete with how-to lectures and sales of sexual appliances for every imaginable taste, and some not so imaginable. A premier hotel chain invites young couples, clearly college kids in the ads, to check in anytime for a quickie. But the promised bliss? Not here. Not now.

Instead, if you survey the relations between the sexes today, what you see after all the coupling is a profound sadness. In the world of low-commitment sex, cohabitation has replaced marriage for many, and relationships are temporary, leaving the partners mistrustful, resentful, even vengeful once the breakup occurs. Women especially are angriest in the post-revolutionary regime, even though feminists were among the sexual revolution's most vociferous advocates. Many leave their teens already mistrustful after their experience so far. By thirty-five or forty, after another failed relationship, perhaps with a child or two to support and raise, struggling with indifferent success to stay trim and fit to attract another man whom someone ten years younger and fifteen pounds slimmer might also fancy, who could blame a woman for feeling that she has gotten a cosmically raw deal? For black women, the deal is rawer still: for them, sexual liberation has meant even lower low-commitment relationships.

Our liberation has left us lonelier. As modern sex has taken us beyond the realm of love, with its unfree dependency and self-surrender, into a realm of freedom and self-fulfillment, where we can "find ourselves" by "exploring our sexuality," the other person increasingly becomes just a means for us, an appliance interchangeable with any other. So too often we remain alone even when we are most intimately connected, merely using each other for our self-interested purposes. No wonder men and women have become so wary of each other. They have set out to have sex without feelings, and, since men and women don't live beyond the realm of emotion, they are continually getting hurt as they encounter each other, expecting to give and to get so little beyond the sexual thrill.

Sex didn't get stripped bare of its centuries-old nimbus of mystery, romance, and morality by accident. A series of hugely influential if half-baked advocates, writing and prose-lytizing over the course of a century, convinced the world that unhappiness was the fruit of the social prohibitions surrounding sex, and that, could we only break those taboos—all of them, wherever we could find them—joy would reign supreme, the joy of sex being the highest imaginable of human felicities. Men and women would regain their primal innocence and wholeness. If the desired happiness doesn't result, obviously we haven't broken enough taboos, haven't asserted enough sexual freedom, and should redouble our efforts.

Seconding the efforts of the sex gurus were the social hygienists and sex educators who sought to liberate us through wholesome, practical knowledge, clearing away all the obfuscation and superstition, and turning sex into technique. As we taught our young people the mechanics and the etiquette of unrolling a condom onto a banana or a purpose-built wooden dildo, the hygienists preached, disease, inhibition, and shame would retreat from the human scene, and healthy, guiltless self-assurance would take their place. Recreational sex, decoupled by sound education and the use of technology from procreation and from embarrassment, would usher in a new golden age of constant arousal and constant fulfillment that our advertising has sought to depict ever since, with its gleaming smiles and lithe bodies and suggestive poses amid surroundings that are lush, luxurious, and drenched in sunlight.

But a funny thing happened once we started administering a stiff annual dose of sex ed to our children, beginning in kindergarten. Children became sexualized earlier and earlier, a consequence also of the advertising and entertainment fantasy world that surrounds them and to whose allurements their still-fragile egos are particularly susceptible. Ten- and eleven-year-olds now dance like strippers and dress like hookers, even down to the cosmetics and bikini underpants. Today, one in five American kids has become sexually active before fifteen, and those many years of sex ed, normalizing kid sex, have almost certainly contributed to raising the teen pregnancy rate to its current high level, rather than reducing it. Now pregnant sixth-graders are not at all unheard-of—in other words, pregnant *twelve-year-olds.*

Nor are teens generally finding precocious sex to be the sun-drenched golden age promised by the ads. Quite the reverse: too often it leaves them feeling cold and empty and used while they are still children. One famous recent case in suburban Atlanta, extreme but diagnostic for the tendency of the culture as a whole, disclosed a world of teen sex not out of *The Arcadia* but out of *Lord of the Flies*, with hundreds of mostly upper-middle-class kids, some as young as thirteen, engaging in group orgies of Neronian depravity in their parents' McMansions before Mom and Dad got home from the office. By fourteen or fifteen, having seen it all and more than all, they were hard and disillusioned, overcome with a sense of disgust for themselves and for sex. They had had the prescribed dose of sex ed, of course; they had loving if clueless parents, who, themselves beneficiaries of the sexual revolution, had imparted to them no larger vision of the good life than the prevailing nonjudgmentalism, self-realization, and doing-it-if-it-feels-good. Joining these kids at the extreme edge of sexually disenchanted childhood are the twelve-year-old prostitutes and the sexual assaults by thirteen- and fourteen-year-old boys against girls not yet in their teens. These are extreme cases, to be sure: but you can see them or read about them in the papers in most cities, almost any day.

For ghetto kids, the sexual revolution has wreaked a special kind of damage, especially when coupled with welfare. With parents often not just clueless but effectively absent, and peer pressure toward sex relentless, sexual activity begins even earlier than elsewhere in society, and sexual abuse of girls is even more common. But beyond that, the prevailing expectation is that ghetto girls will get pregnant and have a baby early—out of wedlock, for sure, because in most inner-city communities marriage is dead, and indeed relations between the sexes, outside the bedroom, are mistrustful in the extreme. Everything in the inner-city teen's life approves her choice of unwed pregnancy: her enthusiastic mother and grandmother, themselves husbandless; her school, with its cheery nursery for pupils' babies; and of course her own impulses, since babies are lovable and, to the amazement of the feminists, women want them. But it is this set of life choices that perpetuates the urban underclass, proliferating single-parent families with mothers too immature to provide their babies the cognitive and moral nurture, or the adult example, they need to grow up to be successful citizens.

The mistrust between men and women that saturates the ghetto pervades the rest of society as well, if at a lower wattage. "So, when did you guys all become freaks?" asks a liberated young career woman in the hit TV show, "Sex and the City." "Us?" replies the young man; surely it's women who've become "bizarre." This exchange is a perfect epitaph for the sexual revolution.

Crucial to generating such massive disturbance between the sexes was feminism. At the same time that women's libbers enthusiastically promoted the sexual revolution, claiming the freedom to have sex like men, no strings attached, they also demanded freedom from what came to be called their "socially constructed gender role"—from their traditional duties as wives, homemakers, and mothers, of course, as well as from the feelings that went along with them. These duties and feelings were said to be the products not of any innate female nature but wholly artificial, imposed upon them by social convention fabricated by and for men. If women had been unfree, feminists asserted, it was because men had oppressed them, body and soul. Men were enslavers, batterers, rapists, beasts.

And boys were beasts-in-training, who—since gender roles are socially constructed—could only be saved by being educated to be like . . . girls.

After more than three decades in which this view has reigned as the elite wisdom, wariness and confusion and unhappiness fill the hearts both of men and of women as they encounter each other. Part of the confusion springs from the fact that, in one important sense, "gender identity" is of course not "socially constructed." Men and women have different innate predispositions, imprinted upon them by biology. No amount of educational reprogramming will alter the reality that men are men and women are women, with different biological parts to play in the continuation of our species.

But even more of the confusion springs from feminists' deep misunderstanding of the sense in which our sexual identities really *are* a product of human artifice. The project of civilization has been to humanize the natural realities in which we are inescapably embedded. We turn eating into dining; we turn sex into romance and courtship and love, and conceive our children in marriage; we bury our dead and commemorate them. So men and women do not encounter each other as two animals but as *persons*, as human beings. Yes, any other person of the opposite sex is much like another, interchangeable from the biological point of view; but even so, he or she whom we choose is unique and special and the only one for us: and in our act of choice we transfigure the animal into the personal and meet as two souls, two moral beings, not merely as two intestines rubbing voluptuously together. So in the sex roles mankind has invented, we represent ourselves to each other in an idealized light, as two humans with individual selves, not two wolves or two pigs.

These sex roles, which also protect individuals from being treated by others as objects to use and exploit sexually, are the work of the whole human race. They are perpetuated by all the activities that weave our culture, from art and myth to custom and convention. We don't behave toward each other like the cavemen in the cartoons because we know what is expected of us as men and as women, and we know, further, that we face disapproval and ostracism if we transgress. The sexual revolution's dismantling of stigma, as part of its anything-goes nonjudgmentalism, has left individuals much more exposed to violation, whether from the sexual adventurer who seems to promise more than a one-night stand, or from the pedophile, whose gratifications our nonjudgmentalism increasingly is loath to condemn. And it was the power of convention enforced by stigma that maintained marriage for millennia as the highest realization of our sexual identities and the institution by which we passed our store of cultural capital down across the generations.

But as marriage now increasingly gives way to serial cohabitation or, because of easy and stigma-free divorce, to another form of serial temporary unions, we are losing something of inestimable value. Our children suffer by so often losing the support and protection of their fathers. Our civilization suffers by weakening the family, the institution that socializes the young and forms them into citizens. And all of us suffer when our surrounding culture makes it so much more difficult than ever before to form and maintain the lasting commitments and the enduring love that complete and humanize our individual lives.

These losses are the real harvest of the sexual revolution, which no spasm in the loins, however exquisite, can make up for. And by assessing the extent of the losses, we can begin to think about how we can repair the damage the sexual revolution has wrought.

MODERN SEX

SEX NOW

HOW WE MATE

After years of shows about breaking up, Oprah is moving on to shows about making up. In a recent program she separated her studio audience into two sections—men and women—and invited the sexes to talk to each other across the divide. The women launched into an attack. "Why can't you guys be more vulnerable?" "Why are you afraid to commit?" The men counterattacked. "You're trying to turn us into wimps." "You don't respect us as men." Oprah, always the diplomat, searched for ways to bring the two sides closer together.

Oprah isn't the only one engaged in gender diplomacy. A slew of new books focus on healing men and women's fractured relationships. Barnes & Noble's "Relationships" section overflows with titles like *We; Soul Mates; New Intimacy;* and *How One of You Can Bring the Two of You Together.* John Gray, author of the wildly popular series on gender differences, *Men Are from Mars, Women Are from Venus,* is now intent on uniting the two in *Mars and Venus Together Forever.*

But these peacemaking efforts are too little too late. The war between the sexes is not winding down—hostilities are spreading. Men and women's intimate relationships are antagonistic and troubled. Their unions—formal or informal—are ever shorter and more fragile. Even one-night stands often don't last the night. And conflict is as much a part of intimate life today as roses on Valentine's Day.

The talk-show celebrities and self-help authors don't seem to grasp what lies behind this intimate warfare. The trouble between men and women is not a matter of miscommunication or misunderstanding and thus cannot be resolved by decoding sex differences, practicing communication skills, or learning conflict resolution. The source of the strife runs deeper, in a fundamental and probably permanent change in the way we mate.

Every society has an institutionalized mating system to guide men and women as they pair off. Mating regimes vary across eras and cultures—ranging from stately diplomatic negotiations between families to mock or real bride capture—but each tends to be fairly stable over time. In Western societies the dominant mating regime has long rested on romantic courtship leading to long-lasting marriage. But all that is now changing. Courtship is dying; lasting marriage is in crisis.

But this is only half the story, for we are witnessing one of those rare events in social history: the rise of a new mating regime. Writing in the late 1970s, Lawrence Stone, the distinguished Oxford historian of family life, saw signs that the existing marriage and family order might be giving way to a "new, more loosely structured, less emotionally and sexually cohesive, far more temporary" set of arrangements. Two decades later, his forecast seems to be coming true. Men and women come together for sex and reproduction with far less demanding requirements for cooperation and commitment than in the past.

Key to the new mating regime is the diminished role of marriage. Though the majority of Americans will marry at least once, the marriage rate among unmarried adults has nevertheless declined by a third between 1960 and 1995. And marriage in the new regime looks very different from traditional marriage. It is no longer a nearly universal rite of passage between adolescence and adulthood, since Americans now postpone first marriage until their late twenties (twenty-five is the median age for women, twenty-seven for men). Typically, they live together before they marry or as an alternative to marriage, they exit marriage through divorce rather than death, and they often cohabit again after a divorce. In the new regime, marriage no longer looms like Mount Everest on the landscape of adult life. It is more like a hill that people can choose to climb, up and down, once or twice in a lifetime, or bypass altogether.

Cohabitation, rather than marriage, is the distinctive union of the new mating regime. Almost two-thirds of young adults born between 1963 and 1974 began their partnered lives through cohabitation rather than marriage, compared with only 16 percent of men and 7 percent of women born between the mid-1930s and early 1940s. Children are now increasingly living in families with cohabiting couples. In 1998 about 36 percent of unmarried-couple households included a child under eighteen, compared with 20 percent a decade earlier.

As a result, the status of boyfriend and girlfriend has moved out of the social shadows. Newspapers respectfully identify individuals as boyfriends and girlfriends, as do court and school documents. The most recent edition of *Emily Post's Etiquette* spends pages on how to introduce live-in boyfriends and girlfriends to friends, parents, and teachers and—another sign of the times—how living-together couples should announce their breakup to their children and polite society.

The new regime encompasses how men and women come together, how they break apart, and what happens in the aftermath of a breakup—or, to use the argot of the young, who now live under the new regime: hook up, break up, and get even. The hookup is a brief sexual relationship with no strings or rings attached. It can be shorter than a one-night stand or longer than a fling. It may lead to a living-together partnership. But sooner or later (usually sooner), the hookup ends in betrayal and abandonment and thus to breakup. The breakup is filled with passion in one or both partners. Leave-taking triggers a torrent of hot emotions—anger, jealousy, hatred—followed by competing fantasies of getting back together or getting even. Finally, the fiery passion subsides and the fantasies fade, leaving behind regret and resentment.

The new mating regime has not spread evenly across the society and perhaps never will. Ethnic traditionalists and the religiously orthodox may well adhere to the old ways. The affluent and the well educated will use their resources to minimize costs and maximize benefits of the new arrangements. But so far, the new mating regime seems to have advanced furthest among two socially important and culturally influential groups: the never-married young, particularly those on the lower two-thirds of the socioeconomic scale; and blacks of all ages and socioeconomic levels.

Today's teenagers are the first generation to come of age under the new rules. They know little of romantic courtship and even less about marriage, having seen so few good examples. Gone are friendship rings, double dating, going steady, the slow buildup to the first "I love you," and the anticipation of the first kiss. Gone is any reasonable expectation that a sexual relationship carries with it the promise of marriage. Instead, teens party in comradely coed groups and "hook up" for sex.

The first hookup occurs as early as twelve or thirteen for some adolescents, and by the late teens most boys and girls have had sexual intercourse, as has been the case for the last decade or so. In virtually every culture, first sexual intercourse is a milestone in women's lives, heavy with symbolic and emotional significance. Girls want their "first time" to mean something. But today's sexual hookup is rarely a magic moment. And the fast-growing popularity of oral sex, or "fooling around," as it is now known, is hardly designed to fulfill teenage girls' romantic fantasies. Teenage girls want love, with roses and candlelight, with tender words and gentle gazes under starry skies—not this.

Romantic love is disappearing. Girls are getting more "naked, loss-filled sex," in the words of one teacher, but less love. Researchers at the University of North Carolina studying boy-girl relationships among young teens, for example, found a small percentage of kids who had had sex with a partner but had never kissed, held hands, or said "I love you" to that person.

By the time they leave their teens, many young single women have experienced at least one round of hookup-breakup, and they carry its emotional baggage (not to mention the misery of an occasional sexually transmitted infection) into their twenties. By then, many are wary of men. A colleague of mine recently received a letter from a twenty-four-year-old woman who described herself as a "Christian and not a raving feminist." Her early sexual experiences with men, she wrote, had been so miserable that she had been led to "reject marriage, despise men, and decide to become a single parent."

Whereas fully 93 percent of women born between 1933 and 1942 married before ever living with their partners, today cohabitation precedes over half of all first marriages. Among unmarried women aged twenty-five to thirty-nine, about half have lived with an unmarried partner at some time in the past, and roughly a quarter are currently living with a partner.

Nearly half of the cohabiting unions among couples in this age group include children.

Cohabiting unions are more common among the 70-odd percent of today's twenty-five- to thirty-nine-year-olds who lack a college degree than among college grads. According to University of Chicago sociologist Linda Waite, who has examined cohabiting patterns among young adults, this represents a significant shift: it was college students who pioneered cohabitation during the 1960s and 1970s. But fifteen years later, 45 percent of female high school graduates were cohabiting as a first union, compared with 24 percent of female college graduates.

Recently my colleague David Popenoe and I surveyed attitudes toward cohabitation among a small group of never-married, noncollege, middle-middle-class twentysomethings in New Jersey's suburban Bergen County. These young men and women saw cohabitation as a way of "finding out the truth" about a partner in the daily routine of a shared household. By contrast, the old courtship practices—where couples got to know each other through dating, spending time together, and getting to know each other's families—involved putting up an idealized front, they said. Cohabitation, some said, is also a way to test yourself to find out if you are mature and responsible enough for marriage.

In one particular, however, the attitudes of the men and the women we surveyed differed notably. Women were much more likely to believe that it took only a few months to find out what they needed to know and gauge whether the relationship would lead to something more permanent. The young men said they would be happy to cohabit indefinitely. These beliefs produced clear signs of mistrust. The men thought women were living together to "push for weddings";

the women thought men were cohabiting because "guys want to have their cake and eat it too."

Especially striking among the women in this group was the sharp contrast between their general outlook on life and their past histories with men. Overall these women were happy with their lives and optimistic about their futures. None seemed to suffer from any severe problems or pathologies; all wanted to marry and have kids someday. But their past relationships with men had not been happy. One young woman, while still in high school, had run off with an older man who then ditched her. Another had lived with a man for over a year—until he announced that he was marrying someone else at the end of that week. Two women had had cohabiting relationships of more than a year's duration, which had ended. Several said that they had close friends who had been beaten up or stalked by boyfriends. We asked the women to choose one of two statements that more closely represented their views: "The biggest problem facing young people in their twenties today is getting ahead financially and achieving economic independence" or "The biggest problem facing young people in their twenties today is finding and keeping a loving partner." A majority agreed with the second statement. One young woman added, "It's the keeping that's the hard part."

Because hookup-breakup breeds sexual jealousy, especially an outraged male sexual proprietariness, it can be an incubator of violence. Women are at greatest danger when they seek to break off their intimate relationships or when they have another sexual relationship or both. At the shadowy margins of the hookup-breakup regime, therefore, we find enraged men who stalk, batter, and kill partners who try to leave. In 1992–1993, according to the Justice Department's

National Crime Victimization Survey, current or former boy-friends committed 55 percent of all violent crimes by intimate partners; husbands accounted for 31 percent, and ex-husbands 14 percent. The prevalence of cohabiting unions in the new mating regime is not likely to bring down the level of domestic violence. According to Linda Waite, cohabiting couples are 1.8 times more likely than married couples to report episodes of hitting, shoving, and throwing things, even after controlling for income, race, education, and age.

The female style of getting even in the aftermath of a breakup is less violent and deadly. Women content themselves with revenge fantasies to exorcise their jealousy and anger. In the hugely successful movie *Waiting to Exhale*, one of the hero-ines ends her affair with her lying and cheating lover by dumping a pitcher of ice water in his lap—a postmodern twist on the classic movie revenge of dumping water on a man's head. Popular female buddy movies like *Thelma and Louise* feature more lurid fantasies, including blowing things up and blowing men away. In *Boys on the Side*, a woman takes a base-ball bat to her abusive boyfriend's head, ties him up, and hits the road with two gleeful female buddies.

Greeting-card companies have spotted the new trend. Not long ago American Greetings ran a full-page ad in fashion magazines introducing its male-bashing "Thelma and Louise" cards. The advertisement included a sample greeting card that read: "Men are always whining about how we're suffocating them. Personally, I think if you can hear them whining, you're not pressing hard enough on the pillow."

A new genre of self-help books devoted to the art of female revenge—the dump book—includes such titles as: *Dumped: A Survival Guide for the Woman Who's Been Left by the Man She Loved; The Heartbreak Handbook; Getting Over Him; How to Heal the Hurt by Hating;* and *The Woman's Book of Revenge: Getting*

Even When "Mr. Right" Turns Out to Be All Wrong. The basic message of these books is that getting dumped is now an everyday event, so there is no point in getting depressed every time you break up and risking turning depression into a way of life. Instead, the books counsel, you should learn to master the experience of getting dumped. It's no big deal once you get the hang of it.

Unlike soppy self-help books on divorce, dump literature is playful and funny. Forget all that therapy stuff about grieving and recovery, it counsels. Get a grip on yourself, girl. Get over him by getting even. Turn your pain into anger. "The more you express your anger," writes one author, "the less anxious and depressed you will feel." But don't go doing anything illegal or violent, the dump books warn. Revenge should be witty and original, something like the old art of banter—"smart revenge," the dump books call it. The standard for smart revenge is that it should make women laugh and men fume: try cutting the crotch out of his designer suits, sending all his clothes to the most expensive dry cleaner in town and mailing him the claim check, or stuffing baby shrimp into his curtain rods. One book counsels creating an "Ipcress File" of incriminating evidence—letters, bills, tax returns—and using this file to inspire fantasies of all the harm you could do if you chose. "There are photographs you could send to his new girlfriend if you wanted to," the author chortles.

If this advice sounds like junior high, it should. The pattern of hookup-breakup is adolescent, and perpetually so. Whereas marriage was a rite of passage, escorting young people into the sober responsibilities of adulthood and parenthood, hookup-breakup, with its suspension of adult responsibility, is a cycle. It repeats endlessly. It is for young and old alike. That's why adult children are now asking advice columnist Ann Landers whether it is okay for their visiting sixty-five-year-old mother to sleep in the same bed with her new boyfriend, and why there are dating services and relationship books for the fifty-and-over set.

The hookup-breakup cycle spirals downward. Each successive relationship starts out at a lower level of trust and commitment than the one before. Lower commitment leads to cheating. Cheating leads to lying. Lying leads to mistrust. Mistrust leads to breakup, and so on. And mistrust is almost inevitable, since the hookup-breakup mating regime is so often based on a lie. It requires women to feign a lack of interest in marriage in order to "keep a guy." One seasoned practitioner of breakup explains: "My dates usually liked me because they sensed that I didn't care too much about finding a husband." Since the new regime rewards women for their lack of pickiness about partners, little wonder that we see a growing crowd of estimable women who unerringly fall into bed with losers and louts.

Firmly as the new regime has taken hold among the young, especially the noncollege majority, it is even more advanced among African-Americans. Statistical evidence abounds in Orlando Patterson's essay on the relations between the sexes in his recent book, *Rituals of Blood*, which paints a detailed picture of the intimate lives of black Americans. They are single for much of their lives. A very high percentage will never marry. Their unions are fragile and often fleeting. The first living-together union of black couples is less likely to lead to the altar than the first cohabiting unions formed by white couples. (Sixty-six percent of white women's first cohabiting partnerships result in marriage, compared with 49 percent of black women's.) Those black couples who do marry have extremely high rates of divorce, and those who stick it out have strikingly high levels of marital dissatisfaction. In short, according to Patterson, black men and women have the worst of both worlds, simultaneously the most unpartnered and the most unhappily partnered people in the entire society.

Among blacks, the cycle of hookup-breakup begins earlier and continues well past adolescence. Females begin to have sex at earlier ages than other females, but compared with white and Hispanic teenage girls, black girls are also the most likely to say that they did not want to have sex when it happened.

Black men and women clearly have profoundly different beliefs about infidelity—the No. 1 marriage wrecker. You can see it in their behavior. Among all groups, marital fidelity is rarer among men than women, but for blacks the gap is significantly larger. The percentage of currently married black men who report being unfaithful is two and a half times higher than the percentage of married black women who say they have been unfaithful. NBA basketball superstar Charles Barkley puts it this way: "My wife is married. I'm not." For black women, these differences can lead to embitterment and disaffection from men and marriage. In their twenties, black women place a higher value on marriage than any other group of women in the society, but by the time they have reached the end of their thirties, they are the least likely of all women to have faith in marriage.

Most black women, whether they marry or not, are destined to spend most of their adult lives single, Patterson reports. As for black men, until they reach forty, most will experience long periods as singles or in brief relationships. Black men and women go through life isolated and estranged from each other; according to Patterson, "Afro-Americans are the loneliest of all Americans."

Patterson attributes these mating patterns to slavery and

its long aftermath, which, he argues, permanently damaged relationships between black men and women. When the sexual revolution swept over the nation in the 1960s, it delivered a ferocious blow to these already fragile relationships and precipitated the deluge of divorce, unwed teen pregnancy, and disappearing fathers in black American family life. But the rest of the society may be following the lead of black Americans, with a lag of about twenty-five years. This is certainly the case for unwed childbearing—22 percent of all black births in the mid-1960s, and at the same level for whites by the early 1990s.

Although the black experience suggests that the new mating regime's long-term consequences can be bleak, that regime is vastly appealing to men and women in the short run, and it is important to understand why. All mating regimes offer rewards, and the rewards of this one are substantial. Men and women get to do just what they want—and they can do it largely on their own.

The old marriage bargain called for a monogamous child-rearing partnership that lasted for a long time—ideally, a lifetime. It was a demanding bargain, but it brought certain rewards. Husbands gained exclusive sexual access to a wife and enjoyed the certainty that they were the biological fathers of their wives' offspring. Wives gained access to a husband's financial resources, his paternal investment in their offspring, and the social status and privileges of married motherhood. And children had access to the resources and nurture of both parents until adulthood and even beyond.

Today's mating regime proposes that men and women can pursue their reproductive destinies with only minimal involvement with each other. The new bargain is that neither men nor women must surrender their autonomy or prerogatives. No one is pressured to marry and raise children together. Each sex can pursue its own heart's desire. The rewards of this bargain are clear: men get sex without the ball and chain of commitment and marriage; women get a baby without the fuss and muss of a man around the house.

It is not news that men are thrilled with this new deal. They have always chafed under the marriage bargain. What is new and noteworthy is women's change of heart. They have long invested heavily in marriage, greatly benefiting from its rewards and disproportionately bearing the costs when it sours.

Women are signing on to the new bargain for two reasons. One is the simple and oft-noted fact of their growing economic independence. Because they can generate their own resources through paid work or from the state, women are less likely to seek a man to be a breadwinner. Even when they plan to marry, young women believe that they have to be ready to take care of themselves economically. "Men learn to hate you if you try to live off them," one young single woman in her twenties explained to me.

Women are buying into the bargain for another and more important reason. Increasingly they believe that a woman has a right to have a baby on her own. This idea is historically recent, originating with the sexual revolution and the contraception revolution. Based on a careful investigation of what caused the sharp increase in unwed childbearing in the early 1970s, Brookings Institution economist George Akerlof rejects both welfare and the decline in male jobs as explanations. Instead, he argues, social norms changed because access to legal abortion and the Pill—and, later, the morning-after pill, Depo-Provera, Norplant, and other female contraceptives—gave women the legal and technological means to control their fertility and thus their reproductive destiny.

Akerlof's explanation is part of the story, but of course

technology didn't change social norms by itself. A new ideology of sexual freedom accompanied the new technology, insistent that sex was for recreation rather than procreation. According to proponents of the new sex ideology—with a strange combination of feminists and *Playboy* magazine taking the lead—women should be free to enjoy their bodies and their "sexuality" without any of the procreative consequences of sex. The sexual double standard was profoundly unjust to women; girls should be able to have as much carefree unmarried sex as guys. According to this reasoning, virginity was a burden, modesty a hang-up, and marriage a form of patriarchal oppression. Finally, feminists contended, women were the sole proprietors of their uteruses and thus had the right to make all reproductive decisions on their own.

However, something odd happened on the road to reproductive freedom. Feminist leaders in the sixties assumed that most unwed pregnancies were unwanted. Thus when single women got pregnant, feminists expected that women would exercise their choice by ending the pregnancy. As Gloria Steinem famously urged, women should give birth to themselves and not to a baby. But feminists badly misjudged women's deepest desires. As it has turned out, the liberated single women of the nineties are as crazy for a baby as were the unliberated wives of the fifties. Indeed, amid all the dramatic changes in women's lives in recent decades, the desire for a baby remains constant and consistently strong. Young or old, rich or poor, every woman—from Jodie Foster to a fourteen-year-old in the projects—seems to want one. Some women go through excruciating fertility treatments to conceive. Others take the white-glove approach and pick a sperm donor from a catalog. More commonly, still others get fertilized the old-fashioned way. But whatever the reproductive means to a baby, the end remains the same. A baby is the trophy women most prize.

What pro-choice feminists failed to appreciate was that reproductive choice cut two ways. If single women could choose not to have a child, they could also choose to have a child on their own. If single women had the right to abortion, they also had the right to have and keep their babies. Thus the right not to have a baby became the right to have a baby. The rhetoric of single women's rights to reproductive choice joined the rhetoric of a single mother's right to social approval. "Do you mean to tell me that if you can't find a mate, then it's 'no kids for you!'" an indignant reader from Oklahoma wrote to *People* magazine in response to another reader who objected to the magazine's glorification of Jodie Foster's impending single motherhood. "How dare people judge others for wanting to give a child a wonderful life even if they have not yet found their partner."

Another thing happened on the road to reproductive freedom. Men were liberated from the old bargain that held them responsible for an unwanted pregnancy. Before the contraceptive revolution, a young man who got a girlfriend pregnant came under family and social pressures to marry her and support the family. But shortly after the advent of legal abortion and contraception for unmarried women, the shotgun wedding began to disappear. According to Akerlof, a woman's right to choose enlarged male choice as well. If women had the option to choose to have a baby, men had the option to marry and support the mother and child—or not. Akerlof quotes an Internet contributor to a dad's-rights newsgroup: "Since the decision to have a child is solely up to the mother (see *Roe v. Wade*), I don't see how both parents have responsibility to that child."

At the same time that the new bargain gave men greater freedom to pursue their own interests, it also increased pressures on women to have sex without the promise or expectation of marriage. Akerlof argues that this deal created winners and losers. The losers were the women who had sex and then babies with the old-fashioned expectation that their sex partners would be faithfully committed to them and their offspring.

This idea of a woman's right to bear and raise a baby on her own has gained widespread support, especially among the young. A majority (53 percent) of teenage girls today agree with the statement "Having a baby without being married is a worthwhile life-style"—compared with only 33 percent in 1976. Teenage girls also believe that they can do a great job raising a baby on their own. They are twice as likely as boys to say that one person can raise a child as well as two. But that doesn't mean that teenage boys are clinging to old-fashioned ideas about motherhood and marriage. One study asked teenage boys about their views on the best resolution to a pregnancy for an unmarried girl. Between 1979 and 1995, the percentages recommending marriage, abortion, and adoption all declined substantially, while the percentage suggesting that the mother have the baby and the father help support it increased dramatically, from 19 percent to 59 percent.

The more years a young woman spends as a sexually active single, the more attractive a baby becomes. Writing in *The American Enterprise* magazine, Ivy League psychology professor Kristi Lockhart Keil captures the early panic expressed by one of her college students: "How am I even supposed to find someone to marry? I'm scared of getting AIDS, and half the time guys don't use condoms, and you can't trust what people tell you about who they've had sex with. Sometimes, it seems easier not to get married at all—just get inseminated." The panic increases for twentysomething women who have invested their time and hope in a living-together relationship that didn't work out. By the time many single women enter their thirties, they are resolved to look after their own reproductive interests. They can no longer waste time on another living-together partnership that might fail.

So according to the new mating bargain, men and women each chase their separate reproductive desires and dreams. In the short term, the dreams often come true. Men get sex without strings; women get babies, with or without a husband.

What happens in the long term? Men, for the most part, do fine. They are likely to find mates to take care of them and bear their children. Indeed, male mating patterns are steadily moving from monogamous marriage to serial monogamy. Working stiffs tend to have serial cohabiting partnerships with women who may have their babies or bring other men's children into the union, but who will require little in the way of child-rearing responsibilities from their partners. Masters of the Universe, by contrast, tend to take serial wives and have children in two or three "families." From Nantucket to Aspen, it's easy to spot these paunchy, graying, high-status males, pushing a double stroller of twins with their slim young trophy wives at their sides. Some women make out okay, as well. They marry, have a child or two, work at rewarding jobs, and, after some years of managing children, nannies, and careers, while at the same time trying to get the attention of a self-absorbed husband, finally divorce. "I have enough to do without having to take care of a grown-up baby," they typically explain. After divorce, these women report greater happiness with their lives—and why not? Their children are a source of intimacy, they have satisfying work, and they tend to have strong friendships as well.

But these women are in the minority, for most of the losers

in the new bargain are women. Over time, some single mothers begin to have second thoughts about the mating bargain. A mother and her newborn are caught up in a love relationship that is exclusive and possessive, but as children grow older, single mothers realize they cannot be father as well as mother. Survey evidence is revealing here. Most Americans now believe that a woman can successfully raise a boy on her own, but there's a suggestive difference in the views of parents. Those with a child under six are much more likely to agree that mothers can successfully raise boys alone than are those who have an older child. Apparently the practical experience of raising a child changes parents' earlier conceptions about the sufficiency of maternal nurture.

Some single mothers have the same rude awakening. As soon as their sons begin acting like boys, they start looking for a man. A social worker in a wealthy suburb of Boston reports that the mothers most urgently seeking male mentors for their sons are well-educated single-mothers-by-choice whose darling baby boys have grown into rage-filled teenagers.

Other single mothers go in search of a partner who will take care of them and their children. Nowhere is the difference in mating strategy between single women without children and single mothers more evident than in the personal ads. Nowhere is the difference between youthful enthusiasm for the new mating regime and sober second thoughts more clearly apparent.

Child-free single women in search of a mate describe themselves as "sexy," "fun-loving," "pretty," "babe," "fit," and "passionate." Single mothers resort to adjectives like "full-figured," "medium build," and "weight-proportionate." The two groups seek different attributes in a mate. The singles want a guy who is good-looking, romantic, and likes to have a good time. The single mothers want a man who is "drug-free," "honest," "financially stable," "a steady worker," and plays "no head games." While the single women are assertive about what they want in a relationship, the single mothers are touchingly accommodating: "I'm flexible," a "homebody," "I like to do just about anything." Most poignantly, the single mothers are looking for a father for their children. They want someone "family-oriented" and "good with children."

Unfortunately, single mothers are at a severe competitive disadvantage. Male studs want hot chicks, not a "weight-proportionate" single mom with two little mouths to feed. And the mothers who place personal ads seem to understand and compensate for their loss of advantage. They offer a good deal. They advertise that the children are "almost out of nest" and that they are "financially secure." They avoid the "M" word—a big turnoff—and instead say they are looking for an "LTR," or long-term relationship.

These bargain-basement deals no doubt attract some interest. But the men who apply may not be the "family-oriented, steady-working, drug-free" partners the single mothers seek. A common male ploy is to feign interest in the mother's child to win the mother's sexual favors, and, since single mothers are looking for a father figure, the ploy usually works. But once the man gains sexual access, he may become jealous of the time and affection the mother devotes to her child. Family households with a mother and a boyfriend who is not the biological father of the children pose the greatest risk of child abuse.

In sum, this new mating bargain leaves men and women equally free to pursue their desires, but it does not reward them equally over the long term. Women have been its principal ideological advocates, men its principal beneficiaries.

The new regime's effects on children are unambiguous. It leaves them with family attachments that are shifting and insecure. They have no fathers, or multiple fathers, or "step-father" boyfriends who appear and disappear, and they can make no lasting claim to affection or support from these assorted men. The new bargain substantially increases children's risk of family breakup and its multiple losses. Fully three-quarters of children born to cohabiting parents will see the partnership break up before they reach age sixteen. Only a third of children born to married couples face a similar fate.

Children are also the hostages and victims of intimate warfare. No official category encompasses all the violent crimes against children committed as a concomitant of troubled intimate partnerships, but if there were such a category, it would include infanticide, physical and sexual abuse, and kidnapping. It would certainly include the emotional damage caused by witnessing persistent fighting and hatefulness between parents. And it might also incorporate the more humdrum conflict associated with child custody battles and visitation disputes.

The new mating regime imposes myriad social costs. Some fall upon a public system that increasingly must protect women from their violent partners and care for abused, neglected, and abandoned children. The social costs include an expanded family-court system, stepped-up child-support enforcement efforts, increased mediation and conflict-resolution services in the schools, and more. It's a sign of the times that in West Virginia, fourth-grade Girl Scouts can now earn a merit badge in domestic-violence prevention.

Social costs like these cluster at the extreme outer margins of the emerging mating regime. The regime's more mainstream burdens and penalties are harder to quantify. No index yet exists to measure its psychological toll of loneliness, depression, resentment, and unhappiness. To be sure, the course of true love was never easy, and sexual betrayal, jealousy, and conflict are part of a very old human story. But the new mating regime—which began with the promise of enlarged happiness for all—generates a superabundance of discontent, pain, and misery, something that should be a matter of concern to a society as solicitous of adult psychological well-being as ours.

Some commentators see silver linings in these massed clouds. They point to hopeful, if scattered, signs that courtship and marriage may be staging a comeback. They point to conservatizing trends among some young adults, who want tougher divorce laws and less divorce, and who are slightly more disapproving of premarital sex. They cite cultural dissidents like Wendy Shalit and Danielle Crittenden, whose books defending virginity, modesty, and early marriage have found an eager audience of younger women. They march out the wistful young readers who persuaded advice columnist Ann Landers not to discontinue her occasional "how we first met" series of letters from World War II–generation readers on how their wartime romances led to long and happy marriages. When Landers suggested that her readers might be sick of these stories, young women begged her to keep running them. One college student wrote, "I find these stories sweet and romantic. They show us a time when people weren't afraid to fall in love and trust each other. I dream of something like that happening to me."

Some statistics, too, are moving in a positive direction. For example, the divorce rate has declined slightly from its all-time high in the early 1980s and has stabilized. This is good news, to be sure; but one reason the divorce rate has leveled off is that the rate of marriage and remarriage has declined, and cohabiting unions have increased. Nonetheless, it is possible that we are seeing stirrings of a renewed interest in and dedication to lifelong marriage.

But I doubt it. The constituency for the new mating bargain is too large; it includes men and women of all ages and statuses. By contrast, its opposition is small and weak. Children, who have the strongest motivation to oppose the new bargain, have no voice and increasingly no representation in the society. The new regime enjoys powerful ideological support in both the elite and popular cultures. Support for it remains enthusiastic on college campuses and in women's magazines, in best-selling novels and op-ed commentary. It is as widespread in Western Europe as it is in the United States.

True, some women develop second thoughts. But evidence of their regret is buried deep in the small print of the personal ads.

[1999]

THE "L" WORD:
LOVE AS TABOO

"I can see no trace of the passions which make for deeper joy," wrote Stendhal about Americans in his 1822 essay "Love." "It is as if the sources of sensibility have dried up among these people. They are just, they are rational, and they are not happy at all." Imagine the Frenchman's horror if he could hear today's Americans speak of *l'amour* in what *Mademoiselle* magazine calls this "Post-Idealist, Neo-Pragmatic Era of Relationships." Here is Wanda Urbanska, author of *The Singular Generation*, describing her peers in their twenties: "We . . . do not have affairs, we have 'sexual friendships.' We do not fall in love, we build relationships. We do not date, we 'see' each other." A student quoted in a recent article in the *Vassar Quarterly* adopts the same cool attitude. She doesn't care for the term "boyfriend" or "lover"; she speaks instead of "my special friend with whom I spent lots of quality physical time."

Many critics of popular culture decry its heat. But oddly enough, the familiar displays of sex and violence often go hand in hand with a distinct lowering of the emotional temperature. We are rarely moved by them—and neither are our heroes or stars. They display cool, tough self-sufficiency in each chiseled muscle and sneering put-down. Sure, the bed-hopping may seem sexy at first, but before long its vacant predictability adds up to a big yawn.

Even rock and roll, once a soulful forum for aching, lonely hearts or ecstatic lovers, is now just as likely to rap or croon a message of tough, don't-need-nobody independence. "You gotta be bad," sings Des'ree in a recent top-ten hit; "you gotta be strong; you gotta be hard; you gotta be tough; you gotta be stronger; you gotta be cool." Her counsel finds visual embodiment in fashion ads, such as that for Calvin Klein One unisex perfume—perfume, of all things, the primal sexual lure!—in which a line of grungy young men and women demonstrate, with snarling mouths and pointed fingers, various permutations of seen-it-all exasperation.

The emotional coolness and self-sufficiency of the Neo-Pragmatic Era of Relationships often finds much more easy-going expression than this. Television comedian Jerry Seinfeld portrays the benign, loopy side of casual sexual friendships in his top-rated series. He, his eccentric buddies, and Elaine, an ex-lover who seems more like his twin sister, drift good-naturedly through a landscape of sexual friendships that inspire about the same level of feeling as the tuna sandwiches Jerry's friend George orders at the local coffee shop. In the 1992 movie *Singles*, the theme song, "Dyslexic Heart," evokes the sad confusion of the young and disconnected. "For some people, living alone is a nasty hang," shrugs Cliff, one of the movie's slacker heroes, to a girl unaccountably and unsuccessfully pursuing him. "Not me. I'm a self-contained unit."

Of course, it would be absurd to suggest that romantic love is dead in America. After all, for every "Seinfeld" there's a "Mad About You," a comedy series about a devoted newly-wed couple. And for every Des'ree there's a Beverly DeAngelis, a romance guru who writes self-help best-sellers with titles like *Are You the One for Me?*

Still, if love in America is not dead, it is ailing. It is suffering from the phenomenon historian Peter Stearns describes in his book *American Cool*. American cool disdains intense emotions like grief, jealousy, and love, which leave us vulnerable, in favor of an "emotional style" of smooth detachment. If pop culture gods present an elegant vision of American cool, for ordinary mortals the picture is less glamorous. But the unintended consequences of this banal ideal are the same across the economic spectrum: emotional frustration, alienation, and a sexual scene that recalls the drearier imaginings of Nietzsche or Freud.

American cool goes hand in hand with a profoundly rationalistic vision of human relations, which looks with suspicion on mystery, myth, and strong feeling. Powerful cultural trends have combined to produce this general coarsening and flattening of the sensibilities: feminism, which feared that love and equality were incompatible; the scientific rationalism of experts from the helping professions, who have helped advance what Lionel Trilling called our "commitment to mechanical attitudes toward life"; and, above all, America's fierce individualism, whose ideal is the free and adventurous loner.

The beginnings of the disenchantment of love and the rise of American cool are well worth examining if only to gauge the trade-offs we have made during this era of liberation. We've purchased our freedom from inhibition and guilt with a loan from imagination and fantasy. And to gain the array of pleasure once denied the bourgeois soul, we've paid the price of deep feeling.

Feminists mounted the first significant challenge to love's hold on the American imagination. Romantic love is a myth, they argued, a myth inextricably tied up with women's inequality. It reinforces the idea of separate spheres for the sexes, providing a "consolation," as writer Juliet Mitchell put it, for women's "confinement in domesticity." Further, feminists contended, the ideal of love strengthened the myth of weak, dependent womanhood in need of strong male protection. Though this view got some airing as early as the mid-nineteenth century, it took on angry, raw urgency in the early 1970s in works like Shulamith Firestone's *The Dialectic of Sex* and Marilyn French's *The Women's Room*, which called love a "lie to keep women happy in the kitchen so they won't ask to do what men are always doing." Ti-Grace Atkinson went even further: "The psychopathological condition of love is a euphoric state of fantasy in which the victim transforms her oppressor into the redeemer. . . . Love has to be destroyed." Not just a myth and a dangerous illusion, love was a disease in need of a cure.

Some Victorian feminists offered a cure, or at least an antidote, in the form of what they called "rational love." They advocated an "educated" or "organized" union between men and women, a union based on mutual interests and friendly companionship, with knowledge replacing fantasy, and reason superseding untidy passions like jealousy and obsession. In a similar vein, feminists in the 1920s supported the introduction of college marriage courses aimed at dispelling romantic myths with objective, expert knowledge. Companionate marriage—cemented with shared interests, common background, and sexual pleasure rather than strong emotion—became the new rational ideal.

A health and family-life curriculum that the New Jersey Coalition for Battered Women is developing exemplifies a contemporary version of this ideal. The curriculum sets up a contrast between bad, illusory "romantic love" and good, clearheaded "nurturing love." The latter entails responsibility, sharing, friendship, pleasure, and "strong feelings." But examples of "What Love Isn't" include jealousy, possessiveness, obsession, dependency, and giving yourself up—that is, just about every extreme of feeling that romantic love may arouse.

The feminist view of the myth of love contained a curious, counterproductive misreading of history. For if love served to subjugate women, it did no less to men. In many countries where romantic love has not been institutionalized, men's philandering is winked at while respectable women are kept veiled and hidden. In its first institutional flowering in the guise of medieval courtly love, stylized passion turned the wandering, brutish young men of the day—who might literally rape an unprotected woman as easily as slay that night's dinner—into sensitive, pining poets. The important point altogether ignored by early progressive reformers and feminists was that it was precisely as a powerful way of sublimating the passions that romantic love was a civilizing force. A man in love was a man subdued.

But a man in rational or nurturing love? As Peter Stearns points out, the changing articles of *Esquire* magazine suggest just how compelling men would find "organized," "educated" sharing. In the thirties, *Esquire* endorsed the new companionate marriage recommended by feminists and sociologists, publishing many stories and advice columns exploring what one writer called "Brave New Love" and cautioning against the excesses of romantic passion. But by World War II, the magazine, presaging the arrival of *Playboy*, dispensed with all love talk and got down to the nitty-gritty: sex. *Esquire's* trajectory from love to brave new love to sex suggested that lifting the veil of the illusion of love might reveal not the sweet smile of equal, harmonious sexual relations but the predacious grin of raw impulse.

Doctors and health experts, starting at the turn of the twentieth century, espoused theories that echoed the feminist disdain for passion and fantasy. Inspired by advances in the understanding and treatment of venereal disease, the medical profession argued against Victorian sexual repressiveness and in favor of a demystification of sex. "Sex mystery prevents progress," announced a book by a social hygienist, as progressive reformers devoted to the eradication of venereal disease called themselves. By releasing "sex mystery" from the murky control of priests and superstition and bringing it under the bright light of science, humanity would enjoy health and progress.

For all their innovativeness, the social hygienists were hardly sexual freethinkers; by and large they believed in the Victorian virtues of chastity and self-restraint. But they began a process of the medicalization and rationalization of sex whose basic assumptions continue to control much current thinking on the subject. They believed that sexual desire could yield easily to the discipline of logic and information; hence they became the first to advocate sex education in the schools. They would probably not be surprised to find that today it is still usually taught in health classes. And they introduced what author Barbara Dafoe Whitehead has called the "Scopes trial terms" that continue to make the sex education debate so stubbornly hyperbolic: the scientifically minded, enlightened realists versus the superstitious, religious flat-earthers.

Yet the social hygienists would surely be dismayed by some of what is done in the name of health today. For the idea of rationalized and demystified sex has been stretched to its logical limits, as sex mystery—the dense subject of poets, philosophers, mystics, lyricists, and sacred codes—has given way to sex mechanics.

Nowhere is this robotization of sex more glaring than in the curricula of modern sex educators, the intellectual heirs of the social hygienists. In what may have been a swan song of sexual love in 1959, a sex education manual began: "The end and aim of sex education is developing one's fullest capacity for love." Today nothing could seem more quaint. Most modern sex education programs center on teaching not just health but technical skills—communication skills, decision-making skills, refusal skills, and, of course, condom skills. Some years ago the Massachusetts Department of Public Health produced an AIDS-prevention video in which a hip young nurse distributes flash cards depicting the fourteen stages of condom use. The students get together, look at one another's cards, and decide the proper order—which looks like this: "Talk with Partner," "Decision by Both Partners to Have Sex," "Buy the Condom," "Sexual Arousal," "Erection," "Roll Condom On," "Leave Space at Tip (squeeze out air)," "Intercourse," "Orgasm/Ejaculation," "Hold on to Rim," "Withdraw the Penis," "Loss of Erection," "Relaxation," and, finally, an environmental skill, "Throw Condom Out." Note the goose-step courtship suggested to today's robo-lovers: "Talk with Partner," "Decision by Both Partners to Have Sex."

Today's sex educator sees his demystifying task as ensuring not only that kids have the information necessary to avoid disease and pregnancy but also that they have "healthy" attitudes toward sex. A healthy student is one who is "relaxed" and "comfortable" in the presence of the erotic and can speak of sex in the same tones and with the same lack of emotion he might bring to a discussion of carburetors. Giggling kids who appear to suffer from embarrassment or reticence, sure signs of "anti-sex" attitudes or irrational hang-ups, must undergo a program of desensitization. One exercise I recently heard about at a private school in Brooklyn attempted such a reeducation, much to the dismay of a number of parents: in a fifth-grade class students were required to pronounce the words

for the genitals at increasingly louder volume. Children calcu-
lating math problems in nearby classrooms were serenaded by
their ten-year-old friends yelling, "Penis! Vagina!!"

The push to rationalize and deintensify sexual desire is so
total that some educators even try to reprogram their students' fantasy lives. William A. Fisher, a professor of psychology at the University of Ontario, and Deborah M. Roffman, a
sexuality education teacher at the Park School in Brook-
landville, Maryland, suggest one way to steer fantasies into
conformity with the rational ideal. Because teenagers' sexual
fantasies usually don't involve condoms, Fisher and Roffman
propose, why not show them "fantasy walk-throughs" in stories, videotapes, or plays, where kids like themselves "successfully perform . . . sex-related preventive behaviors." "Such
imagery," they continue, "should enter teenagers' memories
as fantasy-based scripts for personally practicing preventive
behaviors when or if such behaviors are necessary."

Striking the same chilling, Strangelovian tone of scientific
detachment, sex educators object to Hollywood's dream vision of sex not because coupling is ubiquitous or mechanical
but because it is "irresponsible" or "unrealistic," with so few
references to birth control, diseases, or abortion. More "pro-
social messages," according to this line of thinking, would
solve the problem of the hypersexed media.

The examples I've cited are extreme; few children are
treated to classroom exercises precisely like these. Nevertheless, such examples expose the inadequacy of the terms of the
recent culture wars over condom distribution, the Rainbow
curriculum, or the promotion of masturbation as a form of
safe sex. What's happening is not as simple as a contest between enlightened liberals seeking to liberate sexual life from
Puritan repressiveness, and life-denying conservatives who
wish to imprison it in a web of moral and religious restric-

tions. On closer inspection, the sexual liberals turn out to be advancing their own rigid moral strictures. Their Eros lays down an updated Puritan law: pleasure and self-fulfillment, yes; passion, no. The question, it begins to seem, isn't whether a society will codify sexual behavior but how it will do so. "From authority," Philip Rieff has written, "there is no escape"; that authority has simply been transferred from the church to the clinic.

This medicalization of sex has deposed the irrational chimera Love and installed reasonable Health as king. Kids must have "healthy" attitudes; they must make "healthy" decisions. A 1993 Good Housekeeping/CBS poll asked teenagers to give reasons not to have sex. While 85 percent mentioned fear of AIDS or pregnancy, only 4 percent said "not being in love." And although the increasing popularity of abstinence as a value to be taught in the schools may seem like an important shift in the cultural climate, it only perpetuates the medical-scientific mode of sexual thinking. An article entitled "AIDS Disinformation" in *Seventeen* illustrates the problem: "Seventy-eight percent of women are sexually active by age 19," it announces. "This is not to say that abstinence isn't an important option. It is the only way to be 100 percent sure of not getting HIV through sexual transmission."

Conventional wisdom has it that the hypersexed media encourage kids to "fool around." But this half-truth begs the question of where in today's culture a teenager can find any alternative vision, any language for imagining sex as a potentially powerful union. Many parents today mumble something like, "Be careful." Meanwhile, their own behavior is corrosive to the idealistic longings of adolescence. In her book *Erotic Wars*, sociologist Lillian Rubin quotes a promiscuous seventeen-year-old who was twelve when her father left her mother for a younger woman. "I don't want to hear about any of that love stuff," the girl says. "It's garbage, just plain garbage. If a guy wants to make it with a girl, he'll say anything. I just spare them the trouble, that's all. Anyway, what's the big deal?"

Educators second this kind of cynicism when they advise kids only to "talk with partner" or "make healthy, good decisions." On what moral terms should a teen ground this good decision? Here the educators come up empty-handed. A National Guidelines Task Force of sex educators looked into this problem and could offer only platitudes like "Every person has dignity and self-worth" and the priceless "All sexual decisions have effects and consequences." Is it any wonder that kids today, stripped of all spiritualizing ideals and with nothing but dismal "health" to replace them, would shrug and ask, "What's the big deal?"

Love's most powerful enemy may well be America's obsession with individual autonomy. The free, self-contained individual—or "unit," as Cliff puts it in *Singles*—looks with suspicion on emotions that threaten dependence on others, and he celebrates those that glorify his splendid isolation. From this point of view, love might well signal childish weakness. "Clearly, romance can arrive with all its obsession whenever we're feeling incomplete," writes Gloria Steinem in her best-selling 1992 book, *Revolution from Within*. "The truth is that finding ourselves brings more excitement and well-being than anything romance has to offer." Steinem's prissy rejection of powerful feeling echoes that of some of her precursors, the nineteenth-century feminists. But it goes a step further. From her perspective, the problem is not merely that love's urgent desire for the other can shade into out-of-control obsession. It is that this obsession sweeps us away from life's central project: finding ourselves.

Finding ourselves is a complex task these days. It means

not only developing interests and talents but also "exploring" what we have come to call "our sexuality." While sex is an activity or behavior involving another individual, sexuality is a territory of the self. Its logic insists that we are all "self-contained units." Others must not interfere.

Watch Oprah, pick up any academic treatise on "gender," flip through any sex education curriculum, or read any self-help book, and the creed of healthy sexuality will stare you in the face. "Sexuality is much more than 'sex' or 'sexual intercourse,'" explains one sex manual for girls. "It is the entire self as girl or boy or man or woman. . . . Sexuality is a basic part of who we are as a person and affects how we feel about ourselves and all our relationships with others." Though it may affect how we feel about others, it does not necessarily tie us to them, for sexuality is first and foremost a vital arena of self-expression and creativity, a central act in the drama of personal identity. Leah P., married eighteen years and interviewed on a National Public Radio show about sex and marriage, admits she would hesitate to have an affair but insists on her autonomy from any rules or institutions or even relationships: "My sexuality belongs to me. I can take it where I choose to. . . . It doesn't belong to my husband; it doesn't belong to my marriage."

The creed of sexuality demands that the individual "explore" or "develop" her sexuality fully by experimenting with different partners, in different positions, at different times of the day, or in different rooms of the house or office. During the seventies, when the novels of Anaïs Nin and Erica Jong were popular, promiscuity became almost a matter of principle for many women newly liberated from old-fashioned notions of what good girls could and couldn't do. Sexual variety and abundance did not merely promise pleasure; they asserted women's freedom and independence. ("That was the meaning of freedom," thinks Nin's heroine Sabine about a one-night stand in *A Spy in the House of Love*.) And further: to expand one's sexuality was to expand one's very identity.

But if sex is imagined as a meeting of free, autonomous, and creative selves, each engaged in an act of self-exploration, we are left with a problem: the lover—or partner, the current term and one better evoking the situation—is in danger of becoming an object to be used and played with. The connection between partners can then only be imagined as contractual: two free agents voluntarily and conditionally involved in a mutually agreed-upon activity. Some of our best and most disenchanted bureaucratic minds have gotten to work on this, as exemplified by the Fourteen Stages of Condom Use and the now-famous Antioch College sexual harassment code. "Obtaining consent is an ongoing process in any sexual interaction," the code reads. "Verbal consent should be obtained with each new level of physical or sexual conduct in any given interaction. . . . The request for consent must be specific to each act."

Although it ostensibly prizes freedom and pleasure, the creed of "sexuality" instead produces this sort of leaden, bureaucratic vision of sex. Here, unlike the lover willing to risk opening his heart in hopes of joyful union, the partner becomes a skilled negotiator demanding and accepting conditions for his or her personal pleasure. Hence "sexuality" inevitably restrains the emotional, truly personal connection between lovers, stifling what Stendhal called the "passions which make for deeper joy." Central to an age of personal health and fulfillment, "sexuality" flattens as well as enriches the self-contained, autonomous individual. It giveth and it taketh away.

How entirely fitting, then, that the latest terrain of the culture wars is masturbation. The multiple ironies of teaching the joys of masturbation to teenagers were largely lost in the usual Scopes trial terms of the brouhaha—either you are anti-sex and believe masturbation makes your palms hairy, or you believe, as one Los Angeles schoolteacher claimed, it is a "way to sexually express yourself without actually having sex." Not least among those ironies is that masturbation does less to enrich sexual life than to advance the project of rational self-sufficiency. No messy emotions here.

Equally ludicrous, but unfortunately dead serious, is the way in which the primacy of the autonomous, self-contained ego freed from the call of passionate love reveals itself in popular culture. "You can find love if you search within yourself," croons Mariah Carey in her 1994 hit song, "Hero." Accompanied by rich orchestral melodies, the video shows her with the quivering lips and outstretched hands usually associated with deep longing for another. "All I really want is to be happy, but the answer lies in me," sings Mary J. Blige in a more recent hit. Camille Paglia may have said more than she realized when she joked about her own gigantic ego: "There's Tristan and Iseult, Romeo and Juliet, me and me. It's the love affair of the century!"

At times the sadness of American detachment seeps through the glossiest of advice columns. One example appears in last September's YM, a teen magazine, in an article entitled "The Six Love Wreckers (and How to Avoid Them)." Five of the six "love wreckers," those things girls do that chase boys away, involve loving too much. They include: "You're too demanding. . . . You're too jealous. . . . You push for a commitment." "Some guys get really uncomfortable when you try to box them in," warns one expert. "Plus, you risk coming off as desperate and needy." "Get a life! . . . Doing your own thing will make him appreciate you more," barks another author, under the headline "You're too dependent." Adult women get similar advice: pronounces a recent *Cosmopolitan* headline, "Clingy Is Out!"

Jealousy, possessiveness, and dependence are the stuff of our contemporary morality stories. The man in love is neither a hero nor henpecked as he once was; he is now a stalker or wife-abuser, our contemporary villain. Both the mainstream media and teen magazines frequently carry updated gothic tales like "My Ex Tried to Kill Me" or "When a Lover Turns Evil; He Follows You—Spies on You—Loves You to Death." The O. J. Simpson trial fascinates us, in large part because it reminds us of the extremes of these tabooed passions.

In this way, popular culture subverts as well as endorses our tidy scientific-therapeutic view of the human condition. Its current fascination with sadomasochism is a perfect example. A recent article in *New York* magazine cited many examples, including the fashion photos in *Details* magazine, Gianni Versace's 1992 fashion show with supermodel Cindy Crawford in bondage getup, and plotlines on soap operas, including "One Life to Live" and—one for the teen set—"Beverly Hills 90210." Though presented as the next stage in a continuing liberation from outdated taboos, the fascination with S&M barely conceals the misery of the robo-lover. Enthusiasts are quick to affirm that S&M sex is "consensual," but with its chains and whips, handcuffs and muzzles, it offers the "partner" one last, desperate chance at surrendering his hardened, encapsulated ego to strong feeling. These sex toys suggest a perverse, high-tech twist on sexual liberation: the man or woman who wants to be dominated and controlled, to give himself up completely to another.

But this interest in S&M reminds us as well that, especially in a rationalized world where a lover's joy pales into pleasure and his tormented longing into co-dependence, irrational fantasy and intense desire will always bubble up. Kids raised in a world without an enriching myth to humanize the Dionysian demons growling and scratching below the surface of civility and to intensify their attachments to another are not a happy sight. For if some teens have reaped the superficial benefits of the new dispensation's relaxation of traditional taboos, all too many suffer from its shallowness.

For girls, the results are not just the widely reported epidemic of sexually transmitted diseases and unplanned pregnancies. Also evident to many working with these young women is a sense of vacant joylessness. Fifteen-year-olds with ten or even more "partners"—sociologist Lillian Rubin interviewed one sixteen-year-old who said she had "40 or 50"—do not merely fail to find love; ironically, they also fail at the pursuit of pleasure, for they are almost never orgasmic. They promise to become a new generation of embittered women, resentful of men, cynical about love, and ripe for single motherhood.

How could they be otherwise, given the boys they have to contend with? Without any humanizing myth to help quiet the demons, boys have begun to play out the truth of Freud's observation that lust and aggression are deeply intertwined. Reports of young studs "playing rape" in a Yonkers school yard during recess, of nine-year-old sexual harassers and fifth-grade rapists and sodomists, have become too common to pass off as simply anomalous. To be sure, boys have always striven to test their manhood through sexual conquest. But the Spur Posse, a gang of teenage boys from Lakewood, California, are just as surely creatures of a crippled emotional culture. The boys held a contest in which they "hooked up"—a tellingly mechanical phrase—with girls as young as ten. (The winner "scored" sixty-six girls.)

Dispiriting as they are, these examples don't totally capture the emotional alienation of this Post-Idealist, Neo-

Pragmatic Era of Relationships. In his 1979 book *The Culture of Narcissism*, Christopher Lasch described the recent crop of patients seeking therapy, who, unlike the general run of patients in the past, "tend to cultivate a protective shallowness in emotional relations" and who are "chronically bored, restlessly in search of . . . emotional titillation without involvement and dependence." Therapists today continue to find such emptiness and emotional blankness the most common complaint. In the past, love has had the virtue not only of satisfying our longing for profound connection but of lifting us out of mundane life into enchantment. While it may not have straightened the crooked timber of humanity, it respected and nourished its tortuous imagination. Today more than ever, the sources of that nourishment seem indeed to have dried up.

[1995]

SEX, SADNESS, AND THE CITY

If you've heard the hype for HBO's hit comedy series "Sex and the City," you might have assumed that the show celebrates the wonders of sexual liberation for Manhattan single women. Mimi Avins of the *Los Angeles Times* gushes that "the smart women of 'Sex and the City' aren't afraid of their femininity or their appetites," and Mike Duffy writes in the *Detroit Free Press* that the show proves that "smart girls just want to have fun, too." *Newsweek* reports that "'Sex and the City' shows us single women who are anything but desperate. They're looking for men, sure, but it's just shopping, not survival. . . . They're well-dressed, well paid and sexually gratified. . . . As our favorite TV foursome prowls through New York hunting down new men and discarding the old ones like last year's Prada bags, they reinforce this fact: women who make their own money don't have to depend on a man, and they don't have to settle. . . . The women of 'Sex and the City' sleep with whomever they want, max out their credit cards and never have to worry about play-dates or carpools. And they know their married friends aren't having any fun at all."

Is this why the show's second season, which ends this month, garnered more viewers than ever—plus Emmy nominations for outstanding comedy series? Is this why offices everywhere in America are abuzz with opinions on every episode?

According to the ads for the show, yes. From atop her martini-glass perch on subways everywhere, Sarah Jessica Parker, the lovely leading lady of "Sex and the City," stares lustily at New Yorkers as she shows them her naked back—though on the paperback cover of *Sex and the City*, a collection of the *New York Observer* columns by Candace Bushnell that sparked the HBO series, Parker is entirely naked, with only a computer as a fig leaf. In all ads she sports the same unsentimental, self-satisfied expression. An observer could only assume that Parker's character Carrie must be awfully pleased with her state of undress and with her enthusiastic participation in New York's sexual scene. And yet, she isn't. Despite the hype, "Sex and the City" is not about girls who just want to have fun, flaunting their sexual appetites. While promoters offer the show as one more brave step in the sexual liberation of women, leading to ever greater fulfillment, in fact it is a lament for all the things of inestimable value that the sexual revolution has wrecked, in this city and beyond. If Candace Bushnell were a practicing Catholic, she couldn't have produced a more effective proselytizing tool for continence and modesty.

The TV show follows the life of New York sex-columnist Carrie, as she tries to find Mr. Right. Until he shows up, Carrie dates Mr. Big (Chris Noth), a fickle forty-two-year-old who sleeps with her regularly but won't let her leave any of her clothes in his apartment. Her single, mid-thirties friends, PR executive Samantha (Kim Cattrall), art dealer Charlotte (Kristin Davis), and corporate lawyer Miranda (Cynthia Nixon), are all equally unsuccessful in searching for a lifelong mate.

This season's opening episode finds Carrie dating the newest Yankee ballplayer. She recently broke up with Mr. Big for not being able to "commit" to her, and she is hoping to make him jealous. All she accomplishes, though, is to burst into a flood of tears when the new Yankee tries to kiss her. "I'm sorry; this is really embarrassing," Carrie stammers. "I just cried in your mouth. I'm not ready!" Then she commiserates with her friends: "I saw Big, and I completely fell apart!" Everyone is sympathetic.

When she is among her girlfriends, Carrie sarcastically dismisses the possibility of love ("Yeah, love, whooo!"), but when left alone she broods over her miserable romantic history: "Ten years' play in New York, countless dates, five real relationships, one serious, all ending in breakups. If I were a ballplayer, I'd be batting, uh . . . whatever really bad is." Catching a fly ball, she concludes bitterly, seems more likely than catching a relationship that endures.

After dating a bunch of men who turn out to be "freaks," including "the man with no soul" and "the man with two faces," Carrie begins to wonder whether all men are freaks. "Apparently," she observes, "the men in the dating world had devolved since the last time I visited." She finally summons up the courage to ask a man directly, but conversationally, "So, when did you guys all become freaks?"

"Us?" he replies, confused. It's the women who are "bizarre."

Though we are meant to conclude that the sexual free-for-all is bringing out the worst in both men and women, Carrie still hopes for more. She wistfully muses that Manhattan was once, "for millions of our forefathers, the gateway to hope, opportunity, and happiness beyond their wildest dreams. Today that hope is still alive: it's called the first date. On Saturday night every restaurant in lower Manhattan resembles its own little Ellis Island: hordes of single women crowded into a hot, cramped space, and hoping to make it to their final destination, matrimony."

In the next episode, Carrie reunites with Big, and he magnanimously allows her to leave a toothbrush at his apartment. Actually, it's not a whole toothbrush—merely a second toothbrush attachment head for his electric toothbrush, but to Carrie this concession signals victory. Big must be getting ready to marry her very soon.

As the season develops, Carrie experiences some setbacks: a friend asks her to write a poem about love for her wedding, but, since Carrie only knows about sex, she has a tough time summoning enough poetic inspiration. At last she produces something she is proud of, only to see Big walk out of the ballroom and take a cell phone call during her recitation. As if that weren't bad enough, he even refuses to sign a card for the wedding present Carrie has bought (that would require too much commitment on his part). Hurt, but endlessly accommodating, Carrie goes home with him anyway.

Encouraged by Big's awarding her that toothbrush head, Carrie strategically tries to leave some of her personal belongings at his apartment. She has little success—he returns all the items the next day—and by the season's end, Big moves to Paris, without bothering to tell her of his plans until just before he leaves. Carrie offers to follow him, but when he explains that he is no more likely to marry her in Paris than in New York, she furiously resolves never to see him again. Not long after, she starts sleeping with other men again.

She pauses only occasionally to wonder whether she is being true to herself, if she is faking more than just her hair color and bra size: "And then I had a frightening thought. Maybe I was the one who was faking it . . . all these years faking to myself that I was happy being single."

Carrie is the most monogamous of the four women. It's hard to say which of her friends takes the prize for promiscuity, all of them having for the most part given up on the idea of having one boyfriend. Charlotte, the brunette art dealer, sleeps with men she doesn't particularly like, just to get things done around the house. As for the men she does care for, she gives them presents they usually reject: "Whoa, too fast," one exclaims to Charlotte: "Next you move in, and then you hate my music!"

Perhaps this is why, in the second episode of the season, Charlotte gets a puppy as a man replacement: "Charlotte came home to the new male in her life," Carrie's voice-over explains. "Fed up with lonely mornings, cuddle-free nights, and the lack of unconditional love she so longed for, Charlotte decided to take matters in her own hands. She combed the city for the perfect specimen of breeding, style, and trendiness . . . Henry, the perfect dog."

While Carrie is reciting her wedding poem, Charlotte is "hooking up" with a man she just met at the wedding. When he behaves boorishly after sleeping with her, Charlotte is astonished: "Did the last four and a half hours mean nothing to you?" she screams at him across the floor.

Consistently, "Sex and the City" derides women who impulsively jump into bed and then complain about men's bad character. The women in the show, it is clear, have given up the opportunity to get to know these men better. When they don't like what they end up with, you'd think they'd become more discriminating. But they never do.

Pushing forty, blonde PR executive Samantha is the most cynical of the four girlfriends. She instructs the other women that "we're all alone, even when we're with men. My advice to you is to embrace that fact, slap on some armor, and go through life like I do, enjoying men!" Yet later on, even sophisticated Samantha gets duped by a club owner, who misleads her about their future together. William promises Sam he'll invite her to East Hampton for the summer, only to stand her up at their second date. Samantha waits for him "without a book, or a project, or any of her dining-alone armor." William, we are told bitterly, was "one of those men who faked a future to get what he wanted in the present." She bursts into tears and flees the restaurant. "I can't believe I fell for some guy's line," she cries to her buddies. "But sometimes you need to hear a 'we.'"

Still, this epiphany doesn't stop Samantha from sleeping with yet another man she just met. But she stops in mid-embrace and declares, "Wait, I've slept with you before!" "Sure," her partner agrees, "fifteen years ago." "Well, why didn't you say anything?"

Oh, no, Samantha thinks to herself—now she's slept with all the men in Manhattan. Her solution is to hatch a big revenge plan. Her plan, aimed not only at one particular ex but at men in general, is to seduce a man who dumped her, have him fall in love with her again, and then she will dump him before they sleep together.

Unfortunately, Samantha is so distracted by her own feelings for him that she ends up going to bed with him anyway. Her plan completely falls apart when, before she can dump her ex, he dumps her for the second time. In this game, emotions put one at a competitive disadvantage. As the narrator of "Sex and the City" explains, "Samantha hadn't evolved past having feelings."

Miranda is the most feminist of the four, a redheaded corporate lawyer who often flounces off, disgusted with her girlfriends for talking about guys all the time. "How does it happen that four such women have nothing to talk about, other than boyfriends?" She goes for a walk, only to overhear women crying: "And I really thought he liked me, so why didn't he call me?" All the women around her seem to be falling apart. But when Miranda sees her ex-boyfriend on the street, she too loses all composure and hides from him. "After two years . . . I had forgotten how hard it is."

Miranda sleeps around just as much as the other girls, but her most inspired act this season is buying her own apartment. She is reluctant to check the single-woman box on the mortgage documents, though, and she is troubled by the fact that the previous owner, a single woman, had died in the apartment. Her body was not found for a week, and a horrible rumor has it that her cat ate half her face.

Miranda frets all the more when she learns that she has a "lazy" ovary and might never have a baby, but when she does come across men who are genuinely nice—maybe nice enough to be a husband and father—it turns out that she has become too cynical to love them. After Miranda has a one-night stand with a bartender, she is puzzled to hear him say afterward, "That was really special."

"Sure," she replies.

"Can I get your phone number?" he inexplicably continues.

"Why?" she asks.

"So I can ask you for a date," he explains.

Miranda's voice is thick with sarcasm as she tells him, "You don't have to make believe you're going to call."

He finally leaves and encourages her to "stop by at the bar sometime."

"Yeah, great sex. Whatever." She waves him away.

A few days later the bartender shows up at her apartment and tells her, "I like you."

Still suspicious, Miranda replies, "Translation: 'I think you're an easy lay and I'd like to have sex again.'"

He protests that he doesn't mean that at all and wants to take her to dinner.

Miranda explains her philosophy: "I can't have dinner with you; I don't even know you!"

"But you slept with me!"

"That's a different thing."

"Can you maybe think for a second that the other night was special?"

"No. Maybe I slept with too many bartenders."

So during half of the "Sex and the City" episodes, the women complain about insensitive men; for the other half, they coach themselves to imitate such men. The result is that by the time the sensitive men appear on the scene, the women have become insensitive too, and incapable of appreciating them.

This portrayal couldn't be more timely. Susan Faludi, the popular feminist who penned *Backlash* in 1991, has just released *Stiffed*, a book about the "betrayal of American men." In this almost conservative and almost honest critique of the culture, Faludi decries our current mores, which encourage men to "score" with many women instead of providing for one. Our notions of manhood were much healthier, she argues, before World War II.

As for why our masculine ideal has changed for the worse, Faludi offers no compelling explanation. The missing piece of her otherwise accurate assessment is precisely what she is not permitted to say, or her feminist sisters would burn her in effigy: in an era of free sexual favors, women no longer demand that men commit to them, and our no-fault-divorce society doesn't back them up when they do.

One of the reasons the critics have misunderstood "Sex and the City" is that it features frank sexual banter and women who swear just as much, and are just as crude as, the men. On the surface, this seems like a nod to equality, but not when you appreciate what these girls are all swearing at. To be sure, the girls bitterly deconstruct their ex- and current boyfriends' sexual techniques and bodies, but only after their hearts have been broken. Miranda, for instance, refers to her ex-boyfriend as "that asshole I dated a couple of years ago," but then Carrie's voice-over explains, "Miranda used to call Eric the love of her life, until he left her for another woman."

The constant hostility the men and women feel for one another is palpable. The women say, "I can't believe the prick hasn't called." The men announce that they're "just getting over the bitch who broke my heart." Women who aren't pretty are of no use whatever to these men and receive scarcely human treatment. "Do you ever shut the fuck up?" one male character asks such a woman, with typical brutality. For all the frantic coupling, no one seems to be having any fun.

Welcome to the Age of Un-Innocence, as Candace Bushnell put it in her original "Sex and the City" column. "The glittering lights of Manhattan that served as backdrops for Edith Wharton's bodice-heaving trysts are still glowing—but the stage is empty. No one has breakfast at Tiffany's, and no one has affairs to remember—instead, we have breakfast at 7 a.m. and affairs we try to forget as quickly as possible. How did we get into this mess?"

What went wrong, plainly, is that women confused sexual sameness with equality and imagined that competing with men in debauchery was part of their social emancipation. The early feminists never wanted to give up their moral power, and that's why they argued strongly against promiscuity.

In her column, Candace Bushnell presents Samantha as a "New York inspiration," a model of the kind of woman who could survive in such a ferocious sexual landscape. And what does life offer Samantha? "If you're a successful single woman in this city," Bushnell writes, "you have two choices: You can beat your head against the wall trying to find a relationship, or you can say 'screw it' and just go out and have sex like a man." Samantha opts to have sex "like a man," and Bushnell's other women emulate her. But the results aren't much better than beating your head against the wall. "I think I'm turning into a man," says Carrie, describing how, after a recent sexual tryst, she didn't feel anything.

"Well, why the hell should you feel anything?" someone else asks. "Men don't. I don't feel anything after I have sex. Oh sure, I'd like to, but what's the point?"

"We all sat back smugly, sipping tea, like we were members of some special club," Bushnell writes of her unfeeling foursome. "We were hard and proud of it, and it hadn't been easy to get to this point—this place of complete independence where we had the luxury of treating men like sex objects. It had taken hard work, loneliness, and the realization that, since there might never be anyone there for you, you had to take care of yourself."

The publicists and pundits may not get it, but Candace Bushnell and producer Darren Star of the "Sex and the City" TV show understand in their heart of hearts the failure of sexual liberation. That's why all the story lines keep returning to the unhappiness of the players involved. The characters of "Sex and the City" accurately represent what the sexual revolution expects of women, and what the woman who looks for liberation through the bedroom can expect. The writers know that their four protagonists, for all their cool urbanity, experience feelings of loss and sadness and loneliness that are real and typical for women in the age of liberation.

For every incident in "Sex and the City" that may seem like a caricature, you can find a real-life woman in America with an even more extreme story. Take Grace Quek, flatteringly profiled in *Allure* magazine recently because she had had sex with 251 men in a single day and had immortalized her feat in an X-rated "documentary," *World's Biggest Gang Bang*, shown at the 1999 Sundance Film Festival. "Actually," writes *Allure*, Quek's film "satirizes masculinity while expressing the enormity of her own desire. To challenge our gender assumptions, Quek put her body (and psyche) on the line."

Allure also reports that Quek had survived a gang rape years before, "which raises a troubling question: Is her adult-film work a way of punishing herself for that victimization, or of reclaiming her body?" Troubling indeed: for this woman, who takes our culture's standard of liberated womanhood to such lengths, suggests that what our culture expects of all women—to remain indifferent to what is to them most naturally sacred—is really a pathology.

And what our culture considers a pathology is really quite normal. Writing of "Sex and the City" and "Ally McBeal," Stacey D'Erasmo recently wondered in the *New York Times Magazine*: "Why do the sexy, savvy new heroines want nothing so much as rings on their fingers?" Taking for granted that it is weird to want to get married, D'Erasmo answers the question: "The new single-girl pathos seems more like a plea to be unliberated, and fast. These characters really do just want to get married; they just don't want to look quite so naive about it. . . . The new single girl, tottering on her Manolo Blahniks from misadventure to misadventure, embodies in her very slender form the argument that not only is feminism over. It also failed: look how unhappy the 'liberated' woman is! Men don't want to marry her!" And why do women continue to pursue this life of "misadventure"? According to D'Erasmo, "Perhaps, it's because they know . . . that marriage doesn't solve all your problems. It never did."

Sure, the new way of doing things is a mess, goes this line of reasoning, but the old way didn't solve all our problems either. Well, no kidding. But that's like saying that because aspirin doesn't always cure a headache, you are better off banging your head against the wall.

In the second episode of "Sex and the City"'s second season, one woman says sweetly, "I'm a single, thirty-eight-year-old woman, still hoping to get married. I don't want to know the truth." But the next generation, for whom it's not too late, does—and perhaps that's why they enjoy watching "Sex and the City."

[1999]

IDEOLOGY

ALL SEX, ALL THE TIME

If there is one thing of which modern man is utterly convinced, it is that he has reached a state of sexual enlightenment. Gone forever are the days of unhealthy concealment, of absurd Victorian taboos that led to the application of cruel and cumbersome devices to children to prevent masturbation, to prudish circumlocutions about sexual matters, to the covering of piano legs to preserve the purity of the thoughts of men in the drawing room. We are at ease with our sexuality, and the poet Philip Larkin's famous ironic lines

> Sexual intercourse began
> In nineteen sixty-three . . .

express for us an important truth: that for the first time in history we can now enjoy sexual relations without any of the unnecessary social and psychological accretions of the past that so complicated and diminished life. No more guilt, shame, jealousy, anxiety, frustration, hypocrisy, and confusion. Free at last, free at last, thank God Almighty, I'm free at last!

Yet, enlightened as we believe ourselves to be, a golden age of contentment has not dawned—very far from it. Relations between the sexes are as fraught as ever they were. The sexual revolution has not yielded peace of mind but confusion, contradiction, and conflict. There is certainty about nothing except the rightness, inevitability, and irrevocability of the path we have gone down.

A hundred yards from where I write this, twelve-year-old prostitutes often stand under street lamps on the corner at night, waiting for customers. The chief of the local police has said that he will not remove them, because he considers that they are sufficiently victimized already, and he is not prepared to victimize them further (his job, apparently, being to empathize rather than to enforce the law). The local health authorities send a van round several times at night to distribute condoms to the girls, the main official concern being to ensure that the sex in which the girls take part is safe, from the bacteriological and virological point of view. It is the authorities' proud boast that 100 percent of local prostitutes now routinely use condoms, at a cost to the city's taxpayers of $135,000 a year, soon to be increased by the employment of a further outreach worker, whose main qualification, according to the recent job advertisement in the local press, will be "an ability to work non-judgmentally"—that is, to have no moral qualms about aiding and abetting child prostitution. Meanwhile, local residents (such as my neighbors, a banker, a lawyer, an antiquarian bookseller, and two university professors) who object to the presence of discarded condoms in their gardens and in the street outside their homes have been offered a special instrument with which to pick them up, in lieu of any attempt to prevent them from arriving there in the first place. And at the same time, the overwhelming majority of the work done by the social workers of the city concerns the sexual abuse of children, principally by stepfathers and mothers' boyfriends who move in after biological fathers move out.

Evidence of sexual chaos is everywhere. Not a day passes without several of my patients providing ample testimony of it. For example, yesterday I saw a woman who had tried to kill herself after her daughter, nearly sixteen years old, moved out of her home with her eight-month-old child to live with her new twenty-two-year-old boyfriend. It goes without saying that this boyfriend was not the father of her baby but a man she had met recently in a nightclub. The father of the baby was "off the scene," as the end of a liaison is invariably described: fathers round here having their exits and their entrances, their exits usually following their entrances with indecent haste.

The mother was fourteen when the father, age twenty-one, made his entrance. On discovering that she was pregnant, he did what many young men do nowadays in such a situation: he beat her up. This not only relieves the feelings but occasionally produces a miscarriage. In this case, however, it failed to do so; instead the father was caught in flagrante delicto (that is to say, while beating her) by my patient, who promptly attacked him, managing to injure him so severely that he had to go to the hospital. While there, he and she did a little informal plea-bargaining: she would not inform on him for having had sex with an underage girl, if he did not press charges against her for having assaulted him.

My patient subsequently spent what little money she had upon her grandchild's clothes, stroller, crib, bedding, and so on, even going $1,500 into debt to fund its comfort. Then her daughter decided to move out, and my patient was mortified.

Mortified, that is, by the absence of her grandchild, for whom she thought she had sacrificed so much. This was the first objection she had made in the whole affair. She had not considered the sexual conduct of her daughter, or that of either of the two men, to be in any way reprehensible. If the father of her grandchild had not turned violent, it would never have crossed her mind that he had done anything wrong in having sex with her daughter; and indeed, having done nothing to discourage the liaison, she in effect encouraged him.

And her daughter had behaved only as she would have expected any girl of her age to behave.

It might be argued, of course, that such obviously wrongful behavior has occurred always: for when it comes to sexual misdemeanor there is nothing new under the sun, and history shows plentiful examples of almost any perversion or dishonorable conduct. But this is the first time in history there has been mass denial that sexual relations are a proper subject of moral reflection or need to be governed by moral restrictions. The result of this denial, not surprisingly, has been soaring divorce rates and mass illegitimacy, among other phenomena. The sexual revolution has been above all a change in moral sensibility, in the direction of a thorough coarsening of feeling, thought, and behavior.

Watching a British comedy from the mid-1950s recently, I grasped the speed and completeness of that change. In the film was a scene in which the outraged working-class father of a pregnant teenage daughter demanded that the middle-class boy who had made love to her must now marry her. The present-day audience giggled helplessly at this absurdly old-fashioned demand, which only forty-five years previously would still have seemed perfectly normal, indeed unarguable. Such naiveté is not for us in our superior, enlightened state, however, and we prove our sophistication by finding it ridiculous.

But who, one might ask, had the deeper and subtler moral understanding of human relations: the audience of the mid-1950s or that of today? To the 1950s audience it would have been unnecessary to point out that, once a child had been conceived, the father owed a duty not only to the child but to the mother; that his own wishes in the matter were not paramount, let alone all-important, and that he was not simply an individual but a member of a society whose expectations he had to meet if he were to retain its respect; and that a sense of moral obligation toward a woman was not inimical to a satisfying relationship with her but a precondition of it. To the present-day audience, by contrast, the only considerations in such a situation would be the individual inclinations of the parties involved, floating free of all moral or social constraints. In the modern view, unbridled personal freedom is the only good to be pursued; any obstacle to it is a problem to be overcome.

And yet at the same time—in the same audience—there are many young people yearning for precisely the certainties that they feel obliged to mock: young women who hope to find a man who will woo her, love her, respect her, stand by her, and be a father to her children, while there are many men with the reciprocal wish. How many times have I heard from my patients of their aching desire to settle down and live in a normal family, and yet who have no idea whatever how to achieve this goal that was once within the reach of almost everyone!

Our newspapers confirm daily the breakdown of the last vestiges of the traditional mores governing sexual relations. Last weekend, for instance, the British papers reported the third baby born to a homosexual couple by surrogate motherhood, and a liberal paper reported (with implicit approval and admiration, of course) a growing trend among women to make themselves pregnant by artificial insemination, like cattle. Of course, human sexual activity has never been very closely confined to procreation, even before the advent of birth control; but surely this is the first time that procreation has been dissociated from human sexual activity.

Thanks to the sexual revolution, current confusions are manifold. In a society that forms sexual liaisons with scarcely a thought, a passing suggestive remark can result in a lawsuit;

the use of explicit sexual language is de rigueur in literary circles, but medical journals fear to print the word "prostitute" and use the delicate euphemism "sex worker" instead; commentators use the word "transgressive," especially in connection with sex, as a term of automatic approbation when describing works of art, while such sex offenders as reach prison have to be protected from the murderous assaults of their fellow prisoners; anxiety about the sexual abuse of children subsists with an utter indifference to the age of consent; compulsory sex education and free contraception have proved not incompatible with the termination of a third of all pregnancies in Britain and with unprecedented numbers of teenage pregnancies; the effective elimination of the legal distinction between marriage and cohabitation is contemporary with the demand that homosexual couples be permitted to marry and enjoy the traditional legal rights of marriage; and while it has become ever more difficult for married but childless parents to adopt, homosexual couples now have the right to do so. The right of lesbians to artificially aided conception by the sperm of homosexual men has likewise been conceded on the principle of nondiscrimination, and sixty-year-old women naturally enough claim the same rights to in vitro fertilization. Sexual liberty has led to an increase, not to a diminution, in violence between the sexes, both by men and by women: for people rarely grant the object of their affection the freedom that they claim and practice for themselves, with a consequent rise in mistrust and jealousy—one of the great, age-old provokers of violence, as Othello attests. Our era admires sexual athleticism but condemns predatory conduct. Boundaries between the sexes have melted away, as men become women by surgical means, and women men, while demands for tolerance and understanding grow ever more shrill and imperious. The only permissible judgment in polite society is that no judgment is permissible.

A century-long reaction against Victorian prudery, repression, and hypocrisy, led by intellectuals who mistook their personal problems for those of society as a whole, has created this confusion. It is as though these intellectuals were constantly on the run from their stern, unbending, and joyless forefathers—and as if they took as an unfailing guide to wise conduct either the opposite of what their forefathers said and did, or what would have caused them most offense, had they been able even to conceive of the possibility of such conduct.

Revolutions are seldom the spontaneous mass upheaval of the downtrodden, provoked beyond endurance by their miserable condition, and the sexual revolution was certainly no exception in this respect. The revolution had its intellectual progenitors, as shallow, personally twisted, and dishonest a parade of people as one could ever wish to encounter. They were all utopians, lacking understanding of the realities of human nature; they all thought that sexual relations could be brought to the pitch of perfection either by divesting them of moral significance altogether or by reversing the moral judgment that traditionally attached to them; all believed that human unhappiness was solely the product of laws, customs, and taboos. They were not the kind of people to take seriously Edmund Burke's lapidary warning that "it is ordained in the eternal constitution of things that men of intemperate minds cannot be free": on the contrary, just as appetites often grow with the feeding, so the demands of the revolutionaries escalated whenever the last demand was met. When the expected happiness failed to emerge, the analysis of the problem and the proposed solution were always the same: more license, less self-control. By 1994, John Money, perhaps the most influential academic sexologist of the last third of the twentieth century, was still able to write in all seriousness that we live in an anti-sexual and taboo-ridden society. Get rid of the remaining taboos, he implied, and human unhappiness will take care of itself.

Not that there are many taboos left to destroy. In my hospital, for example, adolescent and young adult visitors to their hospitalized boyfriends or girlfriends not infrequently climb into bed and indulge in sexual foreplay with them, in full view of the staff and of old people occupying the beds opposite. This gross disinhibition would once have been taken as a sign of madness but is now accepted as perfectly normal: indeed, objection to such behavior would now appear objectionable and ridiculous. No one seems to have noticed, however, that a loss of a sense of shame means a loss of privacy; a loss of privacy means a loss of intimacy; and a loss of intimacy means a loss of depth. There is, in fact, no better way to produce shallow and superficial people than to let them live their lives entirely in the open, without concealment of anything.

There is virtually no aspect of modern society's disastrous sexual predicament that does not find its apologist and perhaps its "onlie" begetter in the work of the sexual revolutionaries fifty or a hundred years earlier. It is impossible to overlook the connection between what they said should happen and what has actually happened. Ideas have their consequences, if only many years later.

Take the question of adolescent sexuality. It has long been an orthodoxy among the right-thinking that it is perfectly natural and therefore to be welcomed. Any attempt to promote self-control would be killjoy and would drive such sexuality underground once again, resulting in a renewal of furtiveness and yet more teenage pregnancy. That is why British doctors must now connive at illegal sexual acts by distributing contraceptives to underage children without informing their parents.

The patron saint of these ideas is Margaret Mead. In 1928, when she was twenty-seven, she published her *Coming of Age in Samoa*, which made her famous for the rest of her life. When she died fifty years later, her book was still selling 100,000 copies a year. Few university students during that half-century did not read it or at least know its message.

Mead was a pupil of the anthropologist Franz Boas, an extreme cultural determinist who wanted to prove that the angst of adolescence was, like most important human realities, the product of culture, not of biology, as was then generally believed. If a society could be found somewhere in the world in which adolescents felt no angst, QED: hormones were not the cause. Mead, intellectually infatuated with Boas and dependent upon him for her academic advancement, was preordained to find in Samoa what he wanted her to find.

And find it she did—or thought she did. Here was a South Sea paradise in which adolescents spent the years between puberty and marriage in uninhibited sexual activity, as much as possible with as many as possible. There was no jealousy, no rivalry, no anxiety, no guilt, just fun—and, mirabile dictu, no unwanted pregnancy, a somewhat surprising fact that did not arrest Mead's attention then or at any time subsequently. So Mead added a value judgment to Boas's proposition: here was a culture that dealt with sex better than we, as the absence of Samoan adolescent unhappiness proved.

Of course her depiction of Samoa was in error: she was taken in by her ironical informants. Sexual morality in Samoa was puritanical rather than liberal, and owed much to the efforts of the London Missionary Society, no advocate of free love during adolescence or at any other time.

But few people are averse to the message that one can indulge appetites freely without bad consequences to oneself or others, and so Mead's book passed as authoritative. And if youthful sexual libertinism was possible in Samoa with only beneficial social and psychological effects, why not in Sheffield and Schenectady? Even had her depiction of Samoa, *per impossibile*, been accurate, no one paused to wonder whether Samoa was a plausible model for Europe or America or whether the mere existence of a sexual custom—the celibacy of religious communities down the ages, say—should warrant its universal adoption.

So generations of educated people accepted Mead's ideas about adolescent sexuality as substantially correct and reasonable. They took the Samoan way of ordering these matters as natural, enjoyable, healthy, and psychologically beneficial. No doubt Mead's ideas were somewhat distorted as they filtered down into the class of people who had not read her (or any other) book: but it does not altogether surprise me now to meet people who started living in sexual union with a boyfriend or girlfriend from the age of eleven or twelve, under the complaisant eyes of their parents. Only someone completely lacking in knowledge of the human heart—someone, in fact, a little like Margaret Mead—would have failed to predict the consequences: gross precocity followed by permanent adolescence and a premature world-weariness.

For example, an intelligent young woman patient of twenty came to me last week complaining of the dreariness of life. She had given up on education at the age of thirteen to pursue sexual encounters full-time, as it were, but the initial excitement had worn off, leaving only greyness and a vague self-disgust behind. At the time of her induction into the sexual life, of course, she had been led to believe that it was the key to happiness and fulfillment, that nothing else counted:

but as with all monochromatic descriptions of the ends of life, this had proved bitterly disappointing.

And, of course, once boundaries, such as the age of consent, that are to some extent arbitrary but nonetheless socially necessary are breached, they tend to erode entirely. Thus children inhabit a highly sexualized world earlier and earlier, and social pressure upon them to exhibit sexualized behavior starts earlier and earlier. A schoolteacher friend recently told me how she had comforted a seven-year-old who was in tears because a girl in his class had insulted him, calling him a virgin. She asked whether he knew what the word meant.

"No," replied the little boy. "But I know it's something horrible."

The sexual revolutionaries' ideas about the relations between men and women—entailing ever greater sexual liberty, ever less mastery of the appetite—were so absurd and utopian that it is hard to understand how anyone could have taken them seriously. But mere absurdity has never prevented the triumph of bad ideas, if they accord with easily aroused fantasies of an existence freed of human limitations.

One of the earliest of the sexual revolutionaries, the English doctor and litterateur Havelock Ellis, had strong opinions about marriage and relations between the sexes in general. For many years this supremely strange and repulsive, though learned, man—who looked like a tripartite cross between Tolstoy, Rasputin, and Bernard Shaw; who was one of the many semi-pagan ideological nudists that England produced at the end of the nineteenth century; and who never achieved full sexual arousal until his second wife urinated on him in his late middle age—won respect on both sides of the Atlantic as a sexual sage. His works enjoyed immense prestige and wide circulation during the first third of the twentieth century. He attached supreme, almost mystical, importance to the sexual act (perhaps not surprisingly, given his great difficulties with it); his conception of ideal relations between men and women was completely untouched by any awareness of human reality and was at the same time implicitly sordid. Many venerated his views and made them the basis of an entire philosophy of life, as did D. H. Lawrence, another English sexual pagan.

Ellis believed in a complete fusion of two souls that, in the course of the sexual act, would achieve union with the creator of the universe (whom, being a modern pagan, he refrained from calling God). But for this mystical fusion to take place, the relations between men and women first had to be freed of all the dross of petty considerations, such as law, custom, and what was then considered morality. "Our thoughts of duty and goodness and chastity are the things that need to be altered and put aside; these are the barriers to true goodness," Ellis wrote. "I foresee the positive denial of all positive morals, the removal of all restrictions. I feel I do not know what license, as we should term it, may not belong to the perfect state of Man." Once freed from all restraint—social, moral, legal, and political—man would regain his natural beauty and generosity of character. He would become again the noble sexual savage. It never occurred to Ellis and his ilk that he might become instead the prototypical caveman of the cartoonists, dragging off his mate of the moment by the hair.

Ellis was not alone in this adolescent utopian dream of unlimited sex without tears as the key to both human happiness and goodness. Another English doctor who achieved world fame as a sexologist more than half a century later, Alex Comfort, whose sex manuals sold by the tens of millions, was of much the same opinion. Although he apparently had great difficulty in explaining the facts of life to his own son, he advised all fifteen-year-old boys—again, with the notable exception of his own son—to take condoms with them to parties, and he explained to adolescents in his manual *The Facts of Love* that pornography was "a long word for any kind of book or movie about sex which someone wants to prohibit." An anarchist and pacifist who saw all institutions merely as emanations of power, which he believed to be the supreme enemy of human happiness, he had opposed armed resistance to Nazism during World War II. In *Barbarism and Sexual Freedom* (which two phenomena he regarded as diametrically opposed) he wrote: "Normality of the biological kind . . . excludes religious coercion, economic pressure and social custom. Institutions based upon the State and other such bodies, civil or religious, have no place in biological sexuality." In other words, sex should float free from all considerations except the sexual attraction of the moment.

What is left but personal whim in the determination of sexual conduct? It is precisely the envelopment of sex (and all other natural functions) with an aura of deeper meaning that makes man human and distinguishes him from the rest of animate nature. To remove that meaning, to reduce sex to biology, as all the sexual revolutionaries did in practice, is to return man to a level of primitive behavior of which we have no record in human history. All animals have sex, but only man makes love. When sex is deprived of the meaning with which only the social conventions, religious taboos, and personal restraints so despised by sexual revolutionaries such as Ellis and Comfort can infuse it, all that is left is the ceaseless— and ultimately boring and meaningless—search for the transcendent orgasm. Having been issued the false prospectus of happiness through unlimited sex, modern man concludes, when he is not happy with his life, that his sex has not been unlimited enough.

If welfare does not eliminate squalor, we need more welfare; if sex does not bring happiness, we need more sex.

It is a matter of curiosity that such puerile drivel could ever have been mistaken for serious thought; but the fact is that Ellis's and Comfort's view of the proper basis for the relationship between men and women is now the commonly accepted, even orthodox, one. Explaining their decision to part from the mother or father of their children, my patients routinely tell me that they do not experience with her or him the bliss they clearly expected to experience, and that their union had no cosmic significance à la Ellis. The possibility that their union might serve other, slightly more mundane and other-regarding purposes has never occurred to them. That depth of feeling is at least as important as intensity (and in the long run, more important) is a thought completely alien to them. With no social pressure to keep them together, with religious beliefs utterly absent from their lives, and with the state through its laws and welfare provisions positively encouraging the fragmentation of the family, relationships become kaleidoscopic in their changeability but oddly uniform in their denouement.

I have seen Comfort's utopia, and it does not work.

One has only to compare the writings of the sexual revolutionaries with a single sonnet by Shakespeare (to take only one of literature's myriad subtle reflections on love) to see what a terrible retrocession in understanding and refinement those writings represent:

When my love swears that she is made of truth
I do believe her though I know she lies,
That she might think me some untutored youth
Unlearned in the world's false subtleties. . . .
O, love's best habit is in seeming trust,

And age in love loves not to have years told.
Therefore I lie with her, and she with me,
And in our faults by lies we flattered be.

The subtlety of this understanding of the human heart, to say nothing of the beauty with which it is expressed, has never been excelled. Everything is there: the human need for deep companionship throughout life, the inevitability of compromise if such companionship is to last, and the acceptance of the inherent limitations of existence that is essential to happiness. Shakespeare's view answers the needs of man as a physical, social, and spiritual being—and no one with the slightest acquaintance with his work could accuse him of being antisexual.

Another rhetorical technique the sexual revolutionaries favor (apart from the appeal to a fantasy of limitless eroticism) has been to try to dissolve sexual boundaries. They preached that all sexual behavior is, by nature, a continuum. And they thought that if they could show that sex had no natural boundaries, all legal prohibition or social restraint of it would at once be seen as arbitrary and artificial and therefore morally untenable: for only differences in nature could be legitimately recognized by legal and social taboos.

The arch-proponent of this viewpoint was Alfred Kinsey, author of the famous reports, a man who spent the first half of his professional life studying and classifying gall wasps and the second half studying and classifying orgasms: though in the event, he was to find the taxonomy of gall wasps far more complex than that of orgasms, since he came to the conclusion that all orgasms were created equal and endowed by their creator with certain inalienable rights, etc.

Kinsey's program had two pillars, designed to free people of the sexual restraint that he considered the cause of all their miseries. The first was to establish by means of extensive survey that the sexual behavior of Americans was very different from what it was supposed to have been according to traditional morality. Without doubt he skewed his survey to ensure this intensely desired result. He had a personal ax to grind, of course: he was himself a man of perverted sexual appetite, though like most sexual revolutionaries he was a very late developer. He pierced his own foreskin and put metal wires up his urethra, and his filming of two thousand men masturbating to ejaculation (ostensibly to discover how far they could project their semen) must rank as one of history's most prodigious feats of voyeurism.

Having established to his own very great satisfaction that 37 percent of American males had had a homosexual experience leading to orgasm, having expended three times as much space in his report on homosexuality as on heterosexuality, and having intimated that all forms of sexuality lie on a spectrum rather than existing as separate, discrete activities, Kinsey then established the second pillar of his sexual philosophy: what might be termed the Forty Million Frenchmen Can't Be Wrong argument. Our sexual morality, he said, must be based not upon a striving toward goodness, toward an ideal, but upon what actually happens here and now. Otherwise we are merely chasing chimeras. The fact that such a morality extends the scope of what actually happens by providing an instant justification for whatever anybody does whenever he does it appears not to have struck Kinsey; but if it had, it wouldn't have worried him.

Applied in the sphere of financial honesty, Kinsey's argument would have been seen as preposterous at once. A survey of the kind he conducted into financial probity would surely have revealed that there is hardly a person in the world who has never in his life been dishonest—who has never taken so much as a paper clip or overestimated expenses on a tax return. No sensible person would conclude from this that the striving for honesty is a sham, that it is pointless to have any laws regarding financial conduct, that it is perfectly all right for shopkeepers to shortchange their customers and for their customers to steal from them. And yet this is precisely what the sexual revolutionaries, Kinsey foremost among them, have argued in the realm of sex.

The work of dissolving the boundaries continues, never satisfied that it has gone quite far enough—as if to accept one limitation or taboo would be to admit the legitimacy of all. I recently read in a criminological journal that the only conclusive argument against bestiality with chickens was that the chickens were nonconsenting to the liaison, and that therefore their (human? avian?) rights were infringed. And while Kinsey wanted to make all sexual activity equal, psychologist and sex therapist John Money went even further, insisting upon the almost infinite plasticity of what he termed "gender identity." He wrote that "Beyond the four basic reproductive functions [impregnation, menstruation, gestation, and lactation], nothing—nothing—of the differences between the sexes is immutably ordained along sex lines. . . . As long as the four basic reproductive functions are allowed for, . . . no particular gender stereotype is unalterable. A society has almost unlimited choice of role design or redesign." Thus there is no normal and no abnormal either: whatever we choose is good, or at least not bad.

Money became, needless to say, a hero of radical feminists who wished to claim that female "sex roles" had been imposed upon them arbitrarily by society. A self-proclaimed "missionary of sex," who advocated all sex, all the time, he left to each individual the free choice of creating his sexual identity. No perversion was alien to him, pedophilia included, which only those in a state of "moralistic ignorance," he asserted, would condemn. Money became the multiculturalist of sex: with polymorphous perversity replacing cultural diversity as a good in itself.

Money was not only a theoretician but a practitioner, head of the Johns Hopkins Gender Identity Clinic. It was his belief in the unlimited malleability of human sexuality that led him, in his most famous case, to advise the parents of a baby whose penis was nearly cut off during a botched circumcision that he should henceforth be brought up as a girl. After all, what was a girl but a boy in skirts? And what was a boy but a girl given toy guns to play with? The requisite operations once performed on the unfortunate child, to complete what the botched circumcision had nearly accomplished, all would be well.

The boy brought up as a girl continued to show the boylike qualities familiar to any mother. He or she fought like a trooper, was more interested in cars and trains than in dolls, was adventurous and boisterous, and, given a jump rope as a gift, used it only to tie up his or her twin brother. As he or she grew older, he or she expressed no sexual interest whatever in boys. Professor Money continued to describe the case as an unqualified success, and for a long time the scientific and journalistic worlds were fooled. Yes, it was possible to turn little boys into little girls by fiat. No, sexual identity was not fixed by biology but was socially constructed, a product of convention and custom. Money's view was accepted uncritically as true and therefore it became orthodox (I remember being taught it as a medical student).

When at age fourteen the subject of Money's experiment was told of what had happened to him or her in early life, he or she immediately determined to revert to masculinity, for he or she, depressed and maladjusted all through childhood, had known all along in inchoate fashion that something was wrong: and, with yet more reconstructive surgery, he made a sound readjustment to masculinity and is now happily married to a woman. This was a part of the story that Money never told, for it contradicted the philosophy to which he had devoted his entire life's work. It suggested that we cannot construct a sexual utopia of the kind that he, a once-repressed farm boy from New Zealand, had dreamed about.

Such theories could only license and encourage ever more bizarre conduct and appetites, of course. And the escalation of appetite that Jeffrey Dahmer experienced, eventually finding sexual release only in congress with the intestines of his increasing numbers of murdered victims, can occur on a mass scale also, as witness a recent film, funded by the Canadian Arts Council, "normalizing" necrophilia.

And so now, when I meet lesbian patients who have used a syringe full of a male friend's semen to impregnate themselves, they challenge me to dare to pass judgment on them. For who am I to judge what is natural or unnatural, normal or abnormal, good or bad? Transsexuals, in my experience, exude a triumphalist moral superiority, conscious of having forced the world to accept what it previously deemed unacceptable. Perhaps, if they haven't read John Money, they have read the eerily similar opinion of Havelock Ellis, that sexual perversions (which he called "erotic symbolisms") are what most distinguish man from the animals, and are his supreme achievement: "[O]f all the manifestations of sexual psychology, . . . they are the most specifically human. More than any others they involve the potently plastic force of the imagination. They bring us the individual man, not only apart from his fellows, but in opposition, himself creating his own paradise." They constitute the supreme triumph of idealism.

Here is the gnostic reversal of good and evil in the realm of sex, the technique that Sartre and Mailer employed in the realm of criminality, transforming Jean Genet and Jack Abbott into existential heroes. Of course, it is true that human sexuality is different from that of the beasts, but surely not because men can desire intercourse with chickens while chickens cannot reciprocate. We must go to literature, not to sexologists, if we want to understand the difference.

It isn't necessary, of course, for people to read the original sources of ideas for those ideas to become part of their mental furniture. But the ideas and sensibilities of the sexual revolutionaries have now so thoroughly permeated our society that we are scarcely aware any longer of the extent to which they have done so. The Dionysian has definitively triumphed over the Apollonian. No grace, no reticence, no measure, no dignity, no secrecy, no depth, no limitation of desire is accepted. Happiness and the good life are conceived as prolonged sensual ecstasy and nothing more. When, in my work in an English slum, I observe what the sexual revolution has wrought, I think of the words commemorating architect Sir Christopher Wren in the floor of St. Paul's Cathedral: *Si monumentum requiris, circumspice.*

[2000]

SEX ED'S DEAD END

The ninth-grade sex education instructor, says the New York City Board of Ed's HIV/AIDS Curriculum Guide, is to shuffle thirteen index cards, pass them out, and instruct the children to arrange themselves in the proper order, like so: "Buy a latex condom," "Buy a contraceptive foam or lubricant . . . ," "Check to make sure condom package is not torn . . . ," "Check condom expiration date," "Remove condom from package," "Check to see which way the condom unrolls," "Squeeze the tip of the condom to press out air," "Place the condom on the erect penis," "Unroll the condom onto the penis . . . ," "Apply the foam/lubricant," "After ejaculation, hold onto the base of the condom," "Carefully withdraw penis," "Wrap the condom in a tissue or piece of paper and discard." Teachers often call this game "Condom Line-Up."

When the teacher demonstrates how to use a condom, according to the Board of Ed guidelines, she is to stretch it out, explain that "one size fits all," and then unroll it on two of her outstretched fingers. It is certainly a curious exercise, since sexual intercourse with anyone under seventeen constitutes a crime in the state, and those who are enjoined to "buy a condom" are fourteen. However, more fascinating still is the black warning box suspended in mid-page: "Teacher Note," it reads: "Make sure that learning-disabled and all students understand that a condom goes on the erect penis, and not on the fingers as demonstrated."

The imagination is certainly compelled. Is this a common problem? The boy and girl, both fourteen, are obediently conjoining when suddenly the girl recalls what they learned in class that day. "Wait, stop! We aren't practicing safe sex!" The boy fumbles for his crumpled-up jeans beside him and manages to pull out a condom—free, thanks to former chancellor Joseph A. Fernandez. He unrolls it, just as they showed in class. "Is it on your finger?" asks the girl anxiously. "Yeah, don't worry," he reassures her. "Whew," she says, "that was close!"

In the world of the sex educators, you can start talking about AIDS in kindergarten (as the New York mandate directs), and by the tenth year of sex ed, students still will not know how to do it right and do it safely. We are told that kids will "do it anyway" by the very people who assure us in the next breath that kids don't know what they're doing. This stubborn ignorance on the part of our sex education pupils serves an important social purpose. Just think: if kids could do it like their parents did it, without the help of all these educators and coordinators, then a fair number of people would be out of a job.

In New York, five comprehensive health coordinators, one per borough, work for the Board of Education. One of them, Delores Cozier, explained to me that they are the "trainers of trainers." They teach teachers, who in turn teach the teachers who will actually implement the sex education guidelines in their classrooms. The guidelines require teachers to add a sprinkling of sex ed to ordinary lessons. "So if you're teaching *Romeo and Juliet* in literature class," Cozier explains, "the teacher could stop and ask, 'Do you think they practiced safe sex?'"

New York requires every child to take five forty-five-minute sessions of HIV instruction in grades K-6 and six in grades 7-12. Parents can pull their children out of the "methods of prevention" class (i.e., condoms) but not the rest. Under the kindergarten guidelines, "students will learn: the difference between transmissible and non-transmissible diseases; the terms HIV and AIDS; [and] that AIDS is hard to get." Next, the kindergartners learn how people do get it. In first grade they'll learn about new HIV treatments. The guidelines instruct teachers to "hold up [a] picture of Superman or Superwoman" and then tell pupils that, just as Kryptonite weakens Superman, so the HIV virus weakens the body's immune system, but that "new treatments for HIV/AIDS act like Superman's/Superwoman's lead shield." They protect the immune system from the AIDS virus.

However dramatic, this analogy isn't accurate, of course, as the many deaths from AIDS each year will testify. But according to the Curriculum Guide, the point isn't really accuracy but rather the fostering of certain desirable attitudes: "Children need to know that although sexual intercourse can present risks, sexuality is a natural and healthy part of life. HIV/AIDS instruction should not create unnecessary fears about sexuality and sexual intimacy." So AIDS instruction for first-graders includes telling them that, because of the new treatments, they shouldn't worry about acting any differently because of the disease.

Sex ed has become nearly ubiquitous and almost always conveys the same reductive story: sex is all about physical pleasure—and preventing the unwanted effects of pursuing it. Today thirty-seven states and the District of Columbia require schools to provide STD/HIV/AIDS education, and twenty-three states require comprehensive sex education. The basis for many of the current comprehensive programs nationwide is a publication issued by SIECUS, the Sexuality Information and Education Council of the United States, Guidelines for Comprehensive Sexuality Education: Kindergarten–12th Grade.

The guidelines advise that by the time children reach the age of five they be told that "it feels good to touch parts of the body" and that "some men and women are homosexual, which means that they will be attracted to . . . someone of the [same] gender." Latency period, anyone? Not anymore. According to SIECUS, "values inherent in the Guidelines include": that a "sexually healthy adult will appreciate his or her own body," "affirm his or her own sexual orientation," and "enjoy and express his or her sexuality throughout life." Also, he or she will "exercise democratic responsibility to influence legislation dealing with sexual issues." Someone who doesn't vote for a SIECUS-favored candidate, therefore, isn't just a bad citizen; he is sexually unhealthy.

SIECUS lists "Fantasy," "Oral Sex," and "Pleasure" as suggested "sexuality topics for parent-child discussions." "It is normal," reassures Felix E. Gardon, outreach coordinator of SIECUS, "for you to feel uncomfortable talking to your children about sexuality," but you must. "Approaching the issue when your children are still toddlers" is ideal. Gardon even provides some tips for "talking with infants and toddlers (0–2 years)" about sex, making sure they know all the real names of all the parts of their body and so forth. You may be only "0" years old, but since, as the Guidelines state, "all persons are sexual," that includes you.

New Jersey's Family Life program begins its instruction about birth control, masturbation, abortion, and puberty in kindergarten. Ten years ago, when the program started, teachers were uncomfortable with it. According to the coordinator of the program, Claire Scholz, "some of our kindergarten teachers were shy—they didn't like talking about scrotums and vulvas." But in time, she reports, "they tell [me] it's no different from talking about an elbow." In another sex ed class in Colorado, all the girls were told to pick a boy in the class and practice putting a condom on his finger. Schools in Fort Lauderdale, Florida, get a head start on AIDS instruction, teaching it in second grade, four years earlier than state requirements.

It is very strange to be on the receiving end of all this enlightenment, before the onset of sexual awakening. I remember when the sex educator arrived in my fourth-grade Wisconsin public elementary school classroom, carrying a Question Box, with black question marks all over it. It was our learning tool, she explained. Opening the lid, she pulled out a long white slip of paper and cheerily read: "And the first question is . . . 'What is 69?'"

Some boys in the corner giggled. "Now remember, boys and girls," the woman continued, "there is absolutely nothing to giggle about! The first thing we're going to learn in Human Growth and Development is that no question is off limits!" After what seemed like sixty-nine attempts to explain the number 69, I raised my hand: "May I please go to the bathroom?" I hid there for awhile that day.

A week later, in time for our next sex ed class, I arrived at school toting a note from my mother. Thereafter I sat out sex ed in the library. I always felt bad for the girls who didn't have this escape, because after each sex ed session, as the lockers slammed and everyone prepared for the next class, the boys would pick on them, in a strange, new kind of teasing.

"Kelly, do you masturbate?" one boy would say. Then another boy would say, "It's really natural to masturbate, you know." Or: "Why aren't you developing, Kelly? It's time for you to be developing, didn't you hear? You may be a treasure, Kelly, but you ain't got no chest!"

And so on. Invariably, I noticed, just before the girl would burst into tears, she would always say the same thing: "The teacher says that if you tease us about what we learn in class, then you haven't understood the principle of RESPECT." Respect is a very important doctrine in sex education class. Indeed, sex ed teachers often use Respect, a puppet turtle, to teach elementary-school children about their "private places." Unfortunately, the sex ed teacher would be gone by then, so no one really cared about what we had learned from Respect the Turtle.

My public school wasn't unique. In 1993, more than 4,200 school-age girls reported to *Seventeen* magazine that "they have been pinched, fondled or subjected to sexually suggestive remarks at school, most of them . . . both frequently and publicly." Researchers from Wellesley College, following up on the magazine's survey, found "that nearly two-fifths of the girls reported being sexually harassed daily and another 29 percent said they were harassed weekly. More than two-thirds said the harassment occurred in view of other people. Almost 90 percent were the target of unwanted sexual comments or gestures." School officials do very little about this, the Wellesley College researchers also found. One thirteen-year-old girl from Pennsylvania told them: "I have told teachers about this a number of times; each time nothing was done about it."

More recently, psychologist Mary Pipher reports in *Reviving Ophelia* that she is seeing an increasing number of girls who are "school refusers," that is, girls who "tell me they simply cannot face what happens to them at school." One client, Pipher says, "complained that boys slapped her behind and grabbed her breasts when she walked to her locker." Then "another wouldn't ride the school bus because boys teased her about oral sex." Pipher concludes that the harassment that girls experience in the 1990s is "much different in both quality and intensity" from the teasing she received as a girl in the late fifties.

For some reason, no one connects this kind of harassment and early sex education. But to me the connection was obvious from the start, because the boys never teased me—they assumed I didn't know what they were referring to. Whenever they would start to tease me, they always stopped when I gave them a confused look and said, "I have no idea what you guys are talking about. I was in the library." They would almost be apologetic: "Oh, right—you're the weirdo who always goes to the library." And they would pass me by.

But teasing is the least of it. As they confidently promote this early sex education, our school officials are at a loss when it comes to dealing with the new problem of sodomy-on-the-playground. It's hard to keep up with all the sexual assault cases that plague our public schools in any given month. Take only two examples, both reported in the *New York Daily News*: "A 15-year-old girl was sexually assaulted at her Queens high school this week, police said. The victim . . . told cops she was accosted by four teenage boys about 12:45 p.m. Tuesday in a stairwell at Hillcrest High School. . . . While two of the boys stood lookout, the other two sodomized the girl, police said. . . . The attack at Hillcrest occurred less than two weeks after six students were charged in two sodomy attacks on a girl at Martin Luther King Jr. High School in Manhattan" (October 17, 1997).

"Four Bronx boys—the oldest only 9—ganged up on a 9-year-old classmate and sexually assaulted her in a schoolyard, police charged yesterday. . . . .[The girl's mother] said she is furious with Principal Anthony Padilla, who yesterday told parents the attack never happened. . . . The girl's parents and sisters are also outraged that when the traumatized third-grader told a teacher, she was merely advised to wash out her mouth and was given a towel wipe" (October 21, 1997).

The associative link between the disenchanting of sex and increased sexual brutality among children works like this: if our children are raised to believe, in the words of that New Jersey kindergarten teacher, that talking about the most private things is "no different from talking about an elbow," then they are that much more likely to see nothing wrong in certain kinds of sexual violence. What's really so terrible, after all, in making someone touch or kiss your elbow?

It may turn out that the natural embarrassment sex education seeks so prissily to erode points to a far richer understanding of sex than do our most explicit sex manuals. Today those in kindergarten are urged to overcome their "inhibitions" before they have a clue what an inhibition means. Yet embarrassment is actually a wonderful thing, signaling that something very strange or very significant is going on. Without embarrassment, kids are weaker: more vulnerable to pregnancy, disease, and heartbreak.

If "overcoming your embarrassment" is one mantra of sex education, "taking responsibility for your sexuality" is another. The health guidelines for the ninth grade in the Newton, Massachusetts, public schools, called the Student Workbook for Sexuality and Health, inform us that not only do "Sexually Healthy Adolescents . . . decide what is personally 'right' and act on these values," but also they "take responsibility for their own behavior." Grown-ups get the same advice. Author Karen Lehrman warns: "What does undermine feminism is women . . . refusing to take responsibility for their sexuality." Camille Paglia writes: "Every woman must take personal responsibility for her sexuality."

Fine: but if you're a child, you're not sure what taking responsibility for your sexuality entails. And as you grow up, the cult of taking responsibility for your sexuality is essentially a call to action. It inculcates a view of sex that is autonomous and cut off from obligation—whether familial obligation or obligation to one's "sex partner" (as the locution has it).

If "taking responsibility for your sexuality" means "decid[ing] what is personally 'right' and act[ing]" accordingly, that holds true even if what is "right" for you is homosexuality. (The cool postmodern quotation marks around "right" tell us that the term is relative not absolute, subjective not objective—nineties morality through and through.) And sure enough, that's the message the SIECUS fact sheets on "Sexual Orientation and Identity" teach: "SIECUS believes that an individual's sexual orientation—whether bisexual, homosexual, or heterosexual—is an essential part of sexual health and personality. SIECUS strongly supports the right of each individual to accept, acknowledge, and live in accordance with his or her orientation." In other words, pick an orientation and act on it, the sooner, the better.

In Massachusetts's sex ed program, says Ron Barndt, a Newton public high school teacher, there is a "real emphasis on trying to normalize homosexuality." High schools are pressured to create Gay/Straight Alliances, to promote a "healthy relationship between people of different sexual orientations." All over the school, placards read: "Are you aware that 1 out of 10 people are gay?" or, "How do you know what orientation you are?" Former governor William Weld's Commission on Gay and Lesbian Youth recommended that "every High School in Massachusetts which does not have a Gay/Straight Alliance form one."

Last July, Alexander Sanger, president of Planned Parenthood of New York City, penned an op-ed in the *New York Daily News*, "Sex Ed Is More Than Just Saying No: Teens Need All the Facts," explaining why he opposed programs that "preached abstinence." Such programs, he charged, "gag educators rather than teach and empower teens" and therefore "don't merit our money or support." Contends Sanger: "In a perfect world, teenagers would wait until they're older and wiser to have sex. But the fact is, 75 percent of American teens have sex before high school graduation. In New York, more than 54,000 teens, ages 15 to 19, become pregnant each year." Therefore, he concludes, "teens need all the facts."

Where does he think all this high school sex and all these pregnancies are suddenly coming from? Doesn't he find it even a bit curious that the more we do what he prescribes, the more such behavior occurs? Most studies find that knowledge about AIDS or HIV does not decrease risky behavior. A 1988 study in the *American Journal of Public Health*, which examined exactly the year when public health information about AIDS grew, found that no increased condom use among San Francisco's sexually active adolescents resulted. A 1992 study in *Pediatrics* conducted a broader investigation and ended up warning: "It is time to stop kidding ourselves into thinking that our information-based preventative actions are enough or are effective." This shouldn't be so surprising. As New York's sex-ed Curriculum Guide argues explicitly: "Children need to know" that "sexuality is a natural and healthy part of life. HIV/AIDS instruction should not create unnecessary fears about sexuality and sexual intimacy."

The few studies that do demonstrate that sex education changes the behavior of students conclude it is only likely to make them more sexually active. A 1991 study in *Family Planning Perspectives*, for example, found that instruction on contraception was significantly correlated with an earlier onset of sexual activity. Even the Alan Guttmacher Institute, which supports contraceptive-based sex education, notes that teen pregnancy rates have increased 23 percent from 1972 to 1990, and a full one-third of the nation's twenty million STDs yearly strike teens—all during the years comprehensive sex education became widespread.

But beyond this, how does Alexander Sanger imagine he was born if his parents were never given "the facts"? The ground in dispute was never whether we would get the facts—but how and when. Do we get the opportunity to seek out the facts when we are ready? Or do we have them forced upon us when we're not ready, when we're inclined to yawn about the whole thing and conclude it's no big deal? It's really not very complicated why so many kids are getting pregnant these days, now that we have so much sex education on top of a wholly sexualized culture. It's because sex is not a big deal to them, and because they think this is what they are expected to do. They are just trying to be normal kids, to please people like Alexander Sanger and prove that they are "sexually healthy." So not only has sex education failed on its own terms, but it has worsened the problem it was intended to solve.

Sex educators have no shortage of explanations for why their programs don't work. Like the advocates of so many other failed nostrums, they contend that we haven't pushed sex ed hard enough. For example, Randy Sheiner, the Senior Public Health Educator for the New York Department of Health, recently aired his frustration over the New York public schools' condom-distribution program with me. In most schools, he explained, "you have to go all the way to the resource room to get these condoms, and kids might not want to do that. Therefore, the people most at risk, they're not getting their complete education. It flies in the face of self-awareness."

How could we possibly get more "comprehensive" than AIDS education in kindergarten and condom availability in high school? "Woodies," Sheiner replied. "Woodies are wooden models of penises. Without them, it's very hard to know how to put on a condom properly. So far we're not allowed to have them." This if-we-only-had-woodies philosophy seeps through all of sex education. If we were only a little more explicit, a little more perverse, a little less squeamish, then we could finally attain sex education Arcadia: no diseases, no unwanted pregnancies, no hurt feelings, and no obligations.

If sex ed is failing at its primary goal of keeping kids from getting pregnant, how is it doing at its secondary goal of giving them sex lives rich in pleasure and fulfillment? The vision that sex educators inculcate, starting with kindergarten—a vision of autonomous sexuality stripped of all embarrassment—leads to relationships that are utterly disenchanted. The young men and women of my generation don't "make love"; they merely "hook up" when they come together. Here is *Sex on Campus: The Naked Truth About the REAL SEX Lives of College Students*, 1997, explaining the "hookup": "If you realize almost immediately after you finish having sex that this will definitely be a one-time-only event and you really don't want to pursue any relationship—even a purely physical one—with this person, try not to sleep through the night with the person. It may seem awfully awkward and it may be late at night, but get up, get dressed, say, 'Thank you for a wonderful evening,' and go home. . . . Leaving someone with whom you've just traded bodily fluids can seem strange, rude, and inconsiderate, but at least you'll have the knowledge that you were being honest, and it will make things less complicated down the road."

Hookup is my generation's word for having sex (or oral

sex) or sometimes for what used to be called "making out." The hookup connotes the most casual of connections. Any emotional attachment deserves scorn and merits what *Sex on Campus* calls a dangerously high "ball-and-chain rating." It's a strange expression, hooking up—like airplanes refueling in flight: not just unerotic but almost inanimate. Without embarrassment or "hang-ups," we are finding, there cannot be any surrender. We can only hook up.

Sex education failed because it got the reality exactly backward: in fact students are smart and already know how it's done. When young, they look to adults not, pace SIECUS, to explain "fantasy," "oral sex," and "pleasure" to them, but to know what it all means, where it all is leading: that is, they want to know from adults how not to do it. But to those in charge of sex education, abstinence is unrealistic and there's never anything of value in sexual sublimation. At times their kids-will-do-it-anyway ideology even takes on a racialist tinge. As Felix Gardon avers in a recent SIECUS fact sheet, abstinence education "will prove devastating and problematic for low-income communities with Latino, African-American, Asian Pacific and Native American populations." These groups "are involved in sexual behavior" and apparently cannot control themselves. Without sex educators like Gardon toting condoms and showing them the True Safe Way, all would be lost.

New York state law requires sex educators to spend some time discussing abstinence, but it is an incomprehensible notion to them. As Delores Cozier, the Board of Ed's health coordinator, puts it, "Sure, I do believe in abstinence. If you start with a child coming out of the womb, he's abstinent. But after that, abstinence is a choice. The Bible also says you have to procreate. How you gonna procreate if you're talkin' about abstinence?"

It is not hard to see why, in the context of sex education, abstinence is not compelling: it is just one choice out of many—the choice for immature kids, who aren't "ready yet." Little wonder, then, that the Alan Guttmacher Institute found that the abstinence program widely used in California schools "produced only small changes in some teens' sexual attitudes but did not affect the frequency of intercourse or the number of sexual partners."

But programs that present abstinence not in a relativistic way but as the unequivocally right thing to do often succeed. A 1996 Northwestern University Medical School longitudinal study found that 54 percent of the teens who had been sexually active before participating in an abstinence-centered program were no longer sexually active one year later. And whenever Lakita Garth, a former Miss Black California, travels around the country to talk to kids about why they should be abstinent until marriage, she receives a deluge of letters. "The irony of it all is that people say kids don't want to hear an abstinence message, especially these troubled kids," she reports. "But they're actually the most receptive. I couldn't believe the response."

Disenchanted sex hasn't seemed to increase the sum of happiness for my generation, certainly not for the women. We're flocking to Jane Austen movies because we're sick of having the facts shoved in our faces all the time, and we want to be permitted to hope for something more in our lives than all this dreary crudeness. Even in one of its own reports, SIECUS admitted that girls are much less likely than boys to say that they "really feel good about their sexual experiences so far." They are also more likely to say "they were 'in love' with their last sexual partner." The solution to all these romantic disappointments? More sex education.

Yet as time passes and these girls become women, their

pain seems only to grow sharper. The March 1998 issue of *Glamour* magazine, for instance, reports that 49 percent of women wish they had slept with fewer men, compared with 7 percent who wish they had slept with more men and 44 percent who are happy with their number as it is. Those who were happiest with their number were generally those who, like Nina, thirty, had had one partner—her husband. As for the majority of women who were unhappy with their sexual experiences, they were for the most part like Ellen, twenty-nine, who said: "I wish I hadn't given so much of myself—I feel that some of my experiences thinned my soul, and such an effect takes time to undo." She had twenty-three partners. No diseases: presumably she practiced safe sex. Her predicament is one that the sex educators cannot address and, indeed, can only worsen. Her unhappiness comes not from knowing too little but from knowing too much, too soon.

In her 1993 memoir *The Beginning of the Journey*, Diana Trilling describes the simple courtship she had with famed literary critic Lionel Trilling in the late twenties: they dated, they drank cocktails, they argued heatedly over politics. "On Bullfrogs and Alexanders, Lionel and I got to know each other well enough to decide to marry." Six months before their wedding, they went to bed together, she reveals, a fact that caused her deep shame at the time. Would her father find out? It was a radical act, a real risk, "a violation of convention." In her world, "necking was the chief premarital sexual activity." In any case, in six months they married, and after their fifty years together, Trilling says, "I have never met any man to whom I would rather have been married." Though they fought, to be sure, "over a long lifetime, we loved each other very much, . . . and there was never a time or situation in which we could not trust or count on one another."

And yet, and yet . . . after half a century with Lionel and

some two decades as a widow, Trilling wonders: was the hush-hush way her generation treated sex really right? "At seventeen," she writes, "I overheard my mother talking to a woman of a younger and more progressive generation than her own; she was explaining that the sexual ignorance—'innocence' was the word she used—in which she and her contemporaries reared their daughters was designed to preserve their illusions. Was she, I wonder, being honest?"

However reluctant Trilling may be to admit it, though, her illusions were for the most part fulfilled. She could always count on Lionel; she had "never met any man to whom I would rather have been married." Hers is an all-too-common refrain among women of a certain age. They generally take for granted the dating, the courtship rituals, the early marriage they enjoyed, and—what now almost never exists—the lifetime companionship, the simple trust one has with a spouse who is also one's first lover. To them, "innocence" is always in ironic quotes; it was just a word their mothers used. They do not make the connection between this initial innocence and the lasting love that came after. They do not realize that those earnest, highly sublimated political conversations they had are impossible now because adolescents flatter themselves that they are getting right to the point by just having sex. They do not realize that if boys and girls argue seriously at all anymore, they will argue only about the girl's "hang-ups."

And so they wonder, as if trying on a new dress: Hmm . . . maybe I was oppressed? Maybe, in retrospect, the expectation that I be a virgin at marriage was calculated to cheat me out of a good time? They seem to fancy they are being worldly and up to the minute by contemplating such daring thoughts. They have no idea how naive they sound to the women who came after them, who drool over, and would give up their law careers for, the kind of lifelong love Mrs. Trilling describes—

for the kind of world that, at the end of her life, she was so prepared to toss into the garbage bin.

Even SIECUS is starting to realize that all is not well in the world of sex ed. In an astonishing 1997 report, *But Does It Work? Improving Evaluations of Sexuality Education*, SIECUS essentially conceded defeat. A team of experts, fifteen of the "nation's most prominent researchers in sexuality education," concluded in an October 1996 symposium that sex ed hadn't done a thing to reduce teen pregnancy or delay the onset of sexual intercourse. But these goals are "extremely difficult to attain," the panel protested. "Teenage childbearing is affected by many social and economic factors such as poverty, racism, sexism, job opportunities, past history of sexual abuse," and so on. What's more, "changing human behavior is difficult and . . . simple educational efforts themselves have often met with limited success."

We should evaluate sex ed according to different criteria, the panel argues. Proper "evaluations of comprehensive sexuality education should go beyond measuring changes in whether young people are having intercourse, or whether they are using a contraceptive method." (Whenever one hears the word "beyond" in this context, it means that the end of that subject is near, as in, "We need to go beyond students just memorizing their multiplication tables.") "Evaluations of school-based sexuality education should focus on changes in knowledge, attitudes, and skills. Be cautious about measuring outcomes outside the classroom." Be cautious about measuring anything tangible, that is; only measure outcomes that cannot be measured.

Let us give sex education the benefit of the doubt. Let us assume, for the sake of argument, that it is in no way responsible for the rise in teenage pregnancies, that it is in no way blamable for the rise in school sexual assaults, and that it is in

93

no way answerable for the degradation of sex to a mere "hookup." If we accept SIECUS's explanation that sex education has met with "limited success" only because there are simply so many other variables at work, well, isn't that even worse? Why in the world are we spending tax dollars on all these educators, coordinators, and alliances if they don't do a thing? Why are we wasting precious class time on all these programs if indeed "changing human behavior is difficult" and "educational efforts themselves have often met with limited success"?

"Woodies" aside, the simple fact remains that you just can't get any more comprehensive than teaching about AIDS in kindergarten. If that doesn't work, there is nothing left to do but pack up your Question Box and go home.

[1998]

CHILDREN

TWEENS:
TEN GOING ON SIXTEEN

During the past year my youngest morphed from child to teenager. Down came the posters of adorable puppies and the drawings from art class; up went the airbrushed faces of Leonardo di Caprio and Kate Winslet. CDs of Le Ann Rimes and Paula Cole appeared mysteriously, along with teen fan magazines featuring glowering movie and rock-and-roll hunks with earrings and threatening names like Backstreet Boys. She started reading the newspaper—or at least the movie ads—with all the intensity of a Talmudic scholar, scanning for glimpses of her beloved Leo or, failing that, Matt Damon. As spring approached and younger children skipped past our house on their way to the park, she swigged from a designer-water bottle, wearing the obligatory tank top and denim shorts as she whispered on the phone to friends about games of Truth or Dare. The last rites for her childhood came when, embarrassed at reminders of her foolish past, she pulled a sheet over her years-in-the-making American Girl doll collection, now dead to the world.

So what's new in this dog-bites-man story? Well, as all this was going on, my daughter was ten years old and in the fourth grade.

Those who remember their own teenybopper infatuation with Elvis or the Beatles might be inclined to shrug their shoulders as if to say, "It was ever thus." But this is different. Across class lines and throughout the country, elementary and middle-school principals and teachers, child psychologists and psychiatrists, marketing and demographic researchers all confirm the pronouncement of Henry Trevor, middle-school director of the Berkeley Carroll School in Brooklyn, New York: "There is no such thing as preadolescence anymore. Kids are teenagers at ten."

Marketers have a term for this new social animal, kids between eight and twelve: they call them "tweens." The name captures the ambiguous reality: though chronologically midway between early childhood and adolescence, this group is leaning more and more toward teen styles, teen attitudes, and, sadly, teen behavior at its most troubling.

The tween phenomenon grows out of a complicated mixture of biology, demography, and the predictable assortment of Bad Ideas. But putting aside its causes for a moment, the emergence of tweendom carries risks for both young people and society. Eight- to twelve-year-olds have an even more wobbly sense of themselves than adolescents; they rely more heavily on others to tell them how to understand the world and how to place themselves in it. Now, for both pragmatic and ideological reasons, they are being increasingly "empowered" to do this on their own, which leaves them highly vulnerable both to a vulgar and sensation-driven marketplace and to the crass authority of their immature peers. In tweens we can see the future of our society taking shape, and it's not at all clear how it's going to work.

Perhaps the most striking evidence for the tweening of children comes from market researchers. "There's no question there's a deep trend, not a passing fad, toward kids getting older younger," says research psychologist Michael Cohen of

Arc Consulting, a public policy, education, and marketing research firm in New York. "This is not just on the coasts. There are no real differences geographically." It seems my daughter's last rites for her American Girl dolls were a perfect symbol not just for her own childhood but for childhood, period. The Toy Manufacturers of America Factbook states that, where once the industry could count on kids between birth and fourteen as their target market, today it is only birth to ten. "In the last ten years we've seen a rapid development of upper-age children," says Bruce Friend, vice president of worldwide research and planning for Nickelodeon, a cable channel aimed at kids. "The twelve- to fourteen-year-olds of yesterday are the ten to twelves of today." The rise of the preteen teen is "the biggest trend we've seen."

Scorning any symbols of their immaturity, tweens now cultivate a self-image that emphasizes sophistication. The Nickelodeon-Yankelovich Youth Monitor found that by the time they are twelve, children describe themselves as "flirtatious, sexy, trendy, athletic, cool." Nickelodeon's Bruce Friend reports that by eleven, children in focus groups say they no longer even think of themselves as children.

They're very concerned with their "look," Friend says, even more so than older teens. Sprouting up everywhere are clothing stores like the chain Limited Too and the catalog company Delia, geared toward tween girls who scorn old-fashioned, little-girl flowers, ruffles, white socks, and Mary Janes in favor of the cool—black mini-dresses and platform shoes. In Toronto a tween store called Ch!ckaboom, which offers a manicurist and tween singing-star Jewel on the sound system, hypes itself as "an adventure playground where girls can hang out, have fun, and go nuts shopping." A recent article on tween fashion in the *New York Times* quoted one ten-year-old sophisticate primping in a changing room at Saks Fifth Avenue: "It's black and I love to wear black. It goes with everything."

Less cosmopolitan tweens may eschew the understated little black dress, but they are fashion mad in their own way. Teachers complain of ten- or eleven-year-old girls arriving at school looking like madams, in full cosmetic regalia, with streaked hair, platform shoes, and midriff-revealing shirts. Barbara Kapetanakes, a psychologist at a conservative Jewish day school in New York, describes her students' skirts as being about "the size of a belt." Kapetanakes says she was told to dress respectfully on Fridays, the eve of the Jewish Sabbath, which she did by donning a long skirt and a modest blouse. Her students, on the other hand, showed their respect by looking "like they should be hanging around the West Side Highway," where prostitutes ply their trade.

Lottie Sims, a computer teacher in a Miami middle school, says that the hooker look for tweens is fanning strong support for uniforms in her district. But uniforms and tank-top bans won't solve the problem of painted young ladies. "You can count on one hand the girls not wearing makeup," Sims says. "Their parents don't even know. They arrive at school with huge bags of lipstick and hair spray, and head straight to the girls' room."

Though the tweening of youth affects girls more visibly than boys, especially since boys mature more slowly, boys are by no means immune to these obsessions. Once upon a time, about ten years ago, fifth- and sixth-grade boys were about as fashion-conscious as their pet hamsters. But a growing minority have begun trading in their baseball cards for hair mousse and baggy jeans. In some places, $200 jackets, emblazoned with sports logos like the warm-up gear of professional athletes, are de rigueur; in others, the preppy look is popular among the majority, while the more daring go for the hipper style of pierced ears, fade haircuts, or ponytails. Often these tween peacocks strut through their middle-school hallways taunting those who have yet to catch on to the cool look.

Cosmetics companies have found a bonanza among those we once thought of as children. The Tinkerbell Company has sold cosmetics to girls ages four to ten since the late fifties. For the most part, these were really more like toys, props for dress-up games and naive attempts to imitate Mommy. Today Tinkerbell has grown up and gone to Soho. New products for the spring of 1998 included roll-on body glitter and something called "hair mascara," a kind of roll-on hair color, in what the company has described as "edgy colors"—neon green, bright blue, and purple. AM Cosmetics has introduced the Sweet Georgia Brown line for tweens. It includes body paints and scented body oils with come-hither names like Vanilla Vibe and Follow Me Boy. Soon, thanks to the Cincinnati design firm Libby Peszyk Kattiman, after she has massaged her body with Follow Me Boy oil, your little darling will also be able to slip into some tween-size bikini panties.

After completing her toilette, your edgy little girl might want to take in a movie with a baggy-panted, Niked dude. They won't bother with pictures aimed at them, though; nine to twelves are snubbing films like *Madeline* or *Harriet the Spy*. Edgy tweens want cool, hip, and sexy. "When I hear parents complain about no films for their young kids, it kind of gets to me," says Roger Birnbaum, producer of such films for pre-teens as *Angels in the Outfield* and *Rocket Man*, "because when you make those kinds of films, they don't take their kids to see them." They prefer R-rated films like *Object of My Affection*, about a young woman who falls in love with a homosexual; or *Scream*, the horror story about a serial killer hunting down young women; or the soap opera *Titanic*, which succeeded so hugely because teen and tween girls went back to watch three and a half hours of Leonardo di Caprio three, four, even five times. "These are different times," concedes Stanley Jaffe, one of the producers of the new *Madeline*, in response to doubts about the potential of his movie, "and you can't go into it thinking you're making a children's film." In other words, there are no children's movies here.

The same goes for other media. Magazine publishers—by the early nineties magazines like *Sports Illustrated for Kids* and *Nickelodeon* were beginning to replace comics as the print entertainment of choice for children—say that warm and cutesy images are out; cool is in. Celebrities like actor Will Smith and rapper Puff Daddy adorn the cover of almost every issue of *Nickelodeon*, the cable channel's magazine geared toward eight- to fourteen-year-olds. Editor Laura Galen says that whenever her magazine reduces its entertainment coverage, tween complaints flood the mail. By the late eighties, tweens helped launch the new genre of what might be called peach-fuzz rock—bands made up of barely pubescent male sex-symbols-in-training. At that time, girls were going screaming mad for a group called New Kids on the Block; after their voices changed and their beards grew in, New Kids lost out to a group called Hanson, now filling stadiums with panting tweens.

Danny Goldberg, chief executive officer of Mercury Records, which produces Hanson, recalls that teen girls have had immense influence on the music business since the days of Frank Sinatra. "But now," he says, "the teenage years seem to start at eight or nine in terms of entertainment tastes. The emotions are kicking in earlier. It's a huge audience."

No aspect of children's lives seems beyond the reach of tween style. Even the Girl Scouts of America have had to change their image. In 1989 the organization commissioned a new MTV-style ad, with rap music and an appearance by tween lust-object Johnny Depp. Ellen Christie, a media specialist for the organization, said it had to "get away from the uniformed, goody-goody image and show that Girl Scouts are a fun, mature, cool place to be." The Girl Scouts?

Those who seek comfort in the idea that the tweening of childhood is merely a matter of fashion—who maybe even find their lip-synching, hip-swaying little boy or girl kind of cute—might want to think twice. There are disturbing signs that tweens are not only eschewing the goody-goody childhood image but its substance as well.

Tweens are demonstrating many of the deviant behaviors we usually associate with the raging hormones of adolescence. "Ninth and tenth grade used to be the starting point for a lot of what we call risk behaviors," says Brooklyn middle-school head Henry Trevor, as he traces the downward trajectory of deviancy many veteran educators observe. "Fifteen years ago they moved into the eighth grade. Now it's seventh grade. The age at which kids picture themselves starting this kind of activity has gone down."

Hard data about how tweens are defining deviancy down are sketchy. For one thing, most studies of risk behavior begin with fifteen-year-olds. High school kids give fairly reliable answers in surveys, but middle-school kids are often confusingly inconsistent. As for ten-year-olds, until recently it seemed absurd for researchers to interview them about their sexual activity and drug use.

The clearest evidence of tweendom's darker side concerns crime. Although children under fifteen still represent a minority of juvenile arrests, their numbers grew disproportionately in the past twenty years. According to a report by the Office of Juvenile Justice and Delinquency Prevention, "offenders under age 15 represent the leading edge of the juvenile crime problem, and their numbers are growing." Moreover, the crimes committed by younger teens and preteens are growing in severity. "Person offenses, which once constituted 16 percent of the total court cases for this age group," continues the report, "now constitute 25 percent." Headline grabbers—like Nathaniel Abraham of Pontiac, Michigan, an eleven-year-old who stole a rifle from a neighbor's garage and went on a shooting spree in October 1997, randomly killing a teenager coming out of a store; and eleven-year-old Andrew Golden, who, with his thirteen-year-old partner, killed four children and one teacher at his middle school in Jonesboro, Arkansas— are extreme, exceptional cases, but alas, they are part of a growing trend toward preteen violent crime.

Though the absolute numbers remain quite small, suicide among tweens more than doubled between 1979 and 1995. Less lurid but still significant, a London-based child advocacy group called Kidscape announced in March a 55 percent increase over the previous eighteen months in calls reporting tween girl-on-girl bullying, including several incidents involving serious injuries.

The evidence on tween sex presents a troubling picture, too. Despite a decrease among older teens for the first time since records have been kept, sexual activity among tweens increased during that period. It seems that kids who are having sex are doing so at earlier ages. Between 1988 and 1995, the proportion of girls saying they began sex before fifteen rose from 11 percent to 19 percent. (For boys, the number remained stable, at 21 percent.) This means that approximately one in five middle-school kids is sexually active. Christie Hogan, a middle-school counselor for twenty years in Louisville, Kentucky, says: "We're beginning to see a few pregnant sixth-graders." Many of the principals and counselors I spoke with reported a small but striking minority of sexually active seventh-graders.

Equally striking, though less easily tabulated, are other sorts of what Michael Thompson, an educational consultant and co-author of the forthcoming *Raising Cain: Protecting the Emotional Life of Boys*, calls "fairly sophisticated sexual contact" short of intercourse among tweens. Thompson hears from seventh- and eighth-graders a lot of talk about oral sex, which they don't think of as sex; "for them, it's just fooling around," he says. A surprising amount of this is initiated by girls, Thompson believes. He tells the story of a seventh-grade boy who had his first sexual experience when an eighth-grade girl offered to service him in this way. "The boy wasn't even past puberty yet. He described the experience as not all that exciting but 'sort of interesting.'"

Certainly the days of the tentative and giggly preadolescent seem to be passing. Middle-school principals report having to deal with mini-skirted twelve-year-olds "draping themselves over boys" or patting their behinds in the hallways, while eleven-year-old boys taunt girls about their breasts and rumors about their own and even their parents' sexual proclivities. Tweens have even given new connotations to the word "playground": one fifth-grade teacher from southwestern Ohio told me of two youngsters discovered in the bushes during recess.

Drugs and alcohol are also seeping into tween culture. The past six years have seen more than a doubling of the number of eighth-graders who smoke marijuana (10 percent today) and those who no longer see it as dangerous. "The stigma isn't there the way it was ten years ago," says Dan Kindlon, assistant professor of psychiatry at Harvard Medical School and co-author with Michael Thompson of *Raising Cain*. "Then it was the fringe group smoking pot. You were looked at strangely. Now the fringe group is using LSD."

Aside from sex, drugs, and rock and roll, another teen problem—eating disorders—is also beginning to affect younger kids. This behavior grows out of premature fashion-consciousness, which has an even more pernicious effect on tweens than on teens, because, by definition, younger kids have a more vulnerable and insecure self-image. Therapists say they are seeing a growing number of anorexics and obsessive dieters even among late-elementary-school girls. "You go on Internet chat rooms and find ten- and eleven-year-olds who know every [fashion] model and every statistic about them," says Nancy Kolodny, a Connecticut-based therapist and author of *When Food's a Foe: How You Can Confront and Conquer Your Eating Disorder*. "Kate Moss is their god. They can tell if she's lost a few pounds or gained a few. If a powerful kid is talking about this stuff at school, it has a big effect."

What change in our social ecology has led to the emergence of tweens? Many note that kids are reaching puberty at earlier ages, but while earlier physical maturation may play a small role in defining adolescence down, its importance tends to be overstated. True, the average age at which girls begin to menstruate has today fallen from thirteen to between eleven and twelve and a half, but the very gradualness of this change means that twelve-year-olds have been living inside near-adult bodies for many decades without feeling impelled to build up a cosmetics arsenal or head for the bushes at recess. In fact, some experts believe that the very years that have witnessed the rise of the tween have also seen the age of first menstruation stabilize. Further, teachers and principals on the front lines see no clear correlation between physical and social maturation. Plenty of budding girls and bulking boys have not put away childish things, while an abundance of girls with

flat chests and boys with squeaky voices ape the body language and fashions of their older siblings.

"Kids wear sexually provocative clothes at nine because
their parents buy them provocative clothes, not because of
their hormones," Robert L. Johnson, director of adolescent
and young-adult medicine at the University of Medicine and
Dentistry of New Jersey, told me. "A lot of journalists call me
to explain some of these things, and they want a good sound
bite like 'raging hormones' rather than a complex series of social factors."

Of course, the causes are complex, and most people working with tweens know it. In my conversations with educators
and child psychologists who work primarily with middle-
class kids nationwide, two major and fairly predictable
themes emerged: a sexualized and glitzy media-driven marketplace and absentee parents. What has been less commonly
recognized is that at this age the two causes combine to aug-
ment the authority of the peer group, which in turn both
weakens the influence of parents and reinforces the power of
the media. Taken together, parental absence, the market, and
the peer group form a vicious circle that works to distort the
development of youngsters.

Much of the media attention about parents working away
from home for long hours has focused on infants and toddlers,
but the effect of the postmodern domestic routine on a nine- or
ten-year-old merits equal concern. The youngest children,
after all, have continual adult attention, from baby-sitters or
day-care attendants or after-school counselors. But as their
children reach the age of eight or nine, many parents, after
years of juggling schedules and panics over last-minute sore
throats and stomachaches, breathe a sigh of relief as they
begin to see growing signs of competence and common sense
in their youngsters. Understandably concluding that their

children are ready to take more responsibility for themselves, they place a list of emergency numbers on the refrigerator, arrange for a routine after-school phone call, and hand over the keys to the house.

In most people's minds, this sort of arrangement—children alone a few hours after school—is what we mean by latchkey kids. But latchkey kids come in many varieties. According to the educators I spoke with, many youngsters are leaving for school from an empty house after eating breakfast alone. Parents who can afford it will sometimes hand their children three dollars and tell them to pick up juice and a muffin on their way to school. Others have their children pick up fast food or frozen meals for dinner—which a small but sad minority will eat with only Bart Simpson or the local TV newscaster for company.

Almost without exception, the principals and teachers I spoke with describe a pervasive loneliness among tweens. "The most common complaint I hear," says Christie Hogan, "is, 'My mom doesn't care what I do. She's never home. She doesn't even know what I do.'" Although the loneliest and most estranged kids don't talk to counselors and can't even be coaxed into after-school programs when they are available, the more resourceful and socially well-adjusted children stay after school whether or not there is a formal program, hanging around popular teachers and counselors. "We have to shoo them home at six sometimes," recounts one New York City middle-school director. "They don't want to go home. No one's there."

Another, more subtly noxious consequence of the loss of family life has been less commonly understood: the expanding authority of a rigidly hierarchical and materialistic peer group. Kids, like nature, abhor a vacuum, and the power of the school peer group grows luxuriantly in soil left fallow by a rootless home life. With no one home, today's tween is captive to an age-segregated peer group whose inflexible customs and mall-driven ideals are too often the only ones he knows.

Many educators I talked with believe that kids are forming cliques earlier than ever, in the fifth and sixth grades rather than the seventh and eighth, as was the case until recently. Researchers are finding the same thing, as reported, for example, in a recent study published this year entitled *Peer Power: Culture and Identity* by Patricia A. Adler with Peter Adler.

These peer groups should not be confused with simple childhood friendships. They are powerful and harsh mechanisms for making kids conform to the crudest, most superficial values. By late elementary school, according to *Peer Power*, boys understand that their popularity depends on "toughness, troublemaking, domination, coolness, and interpersonal bragging and sparring skills." Girls, on the other hand, "deriv[e] their status from their success at grooming, clothes, and other appearance-related variables; . . . [their] romantic success as measured through popularity and going with boys; affluence and its correlates of material possessions and leisure pursuits." Educators repeatedly note how harsh tweens are toward classmates who wear the wrong brand of sneakers or listen to yesterday's music. Childhood cruelty, always latent, finds an outlet in enforcing the rigid fashion laws of the in-group, whose dominion is now relatively unchallenged by parents and outside peers.

Paradoxically, then, while the tween has less company, he also has less privacy. Hannah Arendt once observed that if you think adults can be authoritarian in their dealings with children, you ought to see the peer group in action. Middle school can be a quasi-Orwellian world, where each child is under continual surveillance by his peers, who evaluate the way he walks, the way he looks, the people he talks to, the number of times he raises his hand in class, the grade he got on his science project. If two kids become romantically linked, their doings are communal property. Each phone call, kiss, or grope is reported, judged, and—in the case of boys, at any rate—simultaneously ridiculed and urged onward by the group leaders. "You kissing her?" they taunt, according to Patricia Hersch in her recent study entitled *A Tribe Apart*. "You get her in bed or something?" Not that things are better if you get rid of the boys. According to one fifth-grade teacher at a private New York City girls' school, students are frequently so wrought up about the vicissitudes of friendships within their group that they can't do their math or English.

Add to this hothouse a glamour- and celebrity-mad tween market-culture, and things get even steamier. In fact, both parental absence and the powerful peer group are intricately connected to the rise of a burgeoning tween market. To be sure, candy, toy, and cereal manufacturers had long known the power of tween cravings before they even defined this new niche group. But tweens really began to catch the eye of businesses around the mid-eighties, a time when, paradoxically, their absolute numbers were falling. The reason was simple. Market research began to reveal that more and more children this age were shopping for their own clothes, shoes, accessories, drugstore items—even for the family groceries.

Jordache Jeans was one of the first companies to spot the trend. "My customers are kids who can walk into a store with either their own money or their mothers'," explained the company's director of advertising at the time. "The dependent days of tugging on Mom or Dad's sleeve are over." Jordache celebrated the new era with ads befitting a revolution. Ignoring—or rather, scorning—parents, they appealed directly to kids who had money in their pockets and puerile dreams of sophistication in their heads. Parents found nothing amusing in seeing jeans-clad youngsters on TV, saying things like

"Have you ever seen your parents naked?" and "I hate my mother. She's prettier than me," and after many complaints, Jordache pulled the plug. Though today's tween ads downplay the shock effect, they take the same fundamental approach: kids are on their own, is the premise; flatter them as hip and aware almost-teens rather than out-of-it little kids—as independent, sophisticated consumers with their own language, music, and fashion.

Anyone who remembers high school will recall many of these dynamics. But it is important to recognize that the combination of isolation from adults, peer cruelty, and fantasies of sophistication, though always a danger to the alienated teenager, is especially taxing to the fragile ego of the preadolescent. With less life experience and even less self-awareness (if that's possible) than their teenage brothers and sisters, preadolescents have fewer internal resources to fall back on. As Helen Colvin, a middle-school science teacher from Harrisburg, Pennsylvania, explains: "These kids have two years less time to become a firm person. That's two years less time to discover what they are, what they believe, to experiment with identity. Instead, they just want to be like their friends."

How do parents view all this? For while they may be out of the house for long hours, parents still have the capacity to break, or at least loosen, the choke hold of the peer group. Many parents negotiate diplomatic compromises, giving in on lipstick, say, while holding the line on pierced navels and quietly trying to present alternatives. But a surprising number of parents, far from seeking to undermine their children's tweenishness, are enablers of it. When Jim Alloy, principal of Fox Lane Middle School in Bedford, New York, tried to ban tank tops, he was beset by a number of irate parents who accused him of discriminating against girls. Other educators marvel at the number of boys whose parents not only buy them expensive Starter jackets but immediately buy them another one if, as so often happens, they lose it.

Many parents are pleased to see their children hip to the market. "I'm glad my girls respond to fashion," said one mother of tweens in a recent *New York Times* article on tween fashion sense. "Trends aren't something you should learn about all of a sudden when you're in college." Another mother frowned over her seven-year-old's choice of a smocked dress as "too babyish." Nor does the enthusiasm for precocity stop with leopard-print tops and thigh-slit black skirts. I sat in amazement at a summer-camp performance this summer as a group of about thirty tweens sang a medley of rock-and-roll songs. The girls in their bare midriffs and mini-skirts shimmied and vamped for the pleasure of their upper-middle-class parents, who whooped and hollered like revelers at a strip joint.

Of course, just because they like rock and roll doesn't mean these parents are trying to push their kids into sex and drugs or, for that matter, alcohol and anorexia. Doubtless many of them are panicky at the prospect of adolescence and all its dangers. Still, their enthusiasm for their children's pseudosophistication betrays a deep confusion about their own role.

The one theme that comes through loud and clear in talking to educators and therapists is that, with parents and their tween children, it's the blind leading the blind. "I'm hearing statements like, 'What can I do? I can't make him read,'" says one director of a New York City private middle school. "And the child is in fifth grade. What does it mean that an adult feels he cannot make a ten-year-old do something?" A middle-school principal from Putnam County, New York, concurs: "I used to say to a kid behaving rudely, 'Young man, would you speak that way at home?' and he would hang his head and say, 'No.' Now I ask a kid, and he looks surprised and says, 'Yeah.'"

It's too simple to trace the trend toward passive parenting back to the time and energy deficits experienced by most working parents. The reluctance to guide and shape tween behavior is as much an ideological as a practical matter. Parents are suffering from a heavy diet of self-esteem talk. In their minds, to force a child to speak politely, to make him read, to punish him for being out of line, is to threaten his most primary need—to express himself. "You'll damage his self-esteem," principals and teachers often hear from parents of children who face discipline for troublemaking.

Though the most influential recent works on preteens and early adolescents, by feminist-inspired child specialists like Carol Gilligan and Peggy Orenstein, focus on girls, they capture the prevailing expert wisdom about self-esteem, whose sorry consequences can be seen in the boorish attitudes of both sexes. According to such experts, the biggest problem tween girls face is not a loss of adult guidance but the opposite. Parents and teachers are guilty of "silencing" girls around this age, goes the argument, and the result is a loss of self-confidence. Instead of submitting children to what Gilligan calls "the tyranny of the nice and the kind," adults should instead focus their parenting energies on supporting and modeling assertive behavior.

And Gilligan and her followers do mean assertive. The new model for girls is the sort of macho, braggart boy that in more levelheaded times made parents hide their daughters. In her study of several California middle schools, Orenstein is impressed by the self-confidence of the boys she observes who call out in class and shout one another down when they have an answer. "[W]hen the girls in [the] class do speak," she writes sadly, "they follow the rules."

Not only did these writers fail to think through what happens when adults believe that children are better off ignoring rules of behavior, but also they neglected to ask about the ultimate purpose of the power they proposed to hand over to children. Confidence, sure—but confidence in the service of what goal? Self-assertion toward what end? Kids certainly couldn't be expected to know the answer. There is nothing in the creed of self-esteem that encourages adults to help mold children's judgment about what matters in life. In fact, quite the opposite. Empowerment implies that children should determine their own style, codes of behavior, and values without serious interference from parents. And they have.

Though the experts missed it entirely, producers of popular culture have been quick to grasp the empty heart of child empowerment, just as they understood the related consequences of parental absence. They saw that children's will to power and immature longings were easy to exploit. Ad writers for Bonne Bell cosmetics, for instance, marry the approved language of self-esteem and the child's natural desire to seem grown-up and hip in the eyes of her peers. "We know how to be cool," goes the text accompanying pictures of a new product called Lip Lix. "We have our own ideas. And make our own decisions. Watch out for us. We are girls."

The Spice Girls, the wildly popular British rock singers who sport slip dresses, hot pants, belly shirts, and oily globs of lipstick and mascara, invented the term "girl power" precisely to evoke the empty formula of self-esteem, whose ingredients are nothing more than self-assertion and face paint—or nothing more than "strength, courage, and a Wonderbra," as one Spice Girl motto puts it. "I'll tell you what I want, what I really, really want," they sing in the tune familiar now to girls five years and older worldwide, girls who at concerts flash the Winston Churchill V-sign and clench their fists in a power salute. And what is it? Caught up in the belief that power was in and of itself a satisfactory guiding virtue, self-esteem theorists failed to consider that what girls might really, really want is to dress up like female impersonators.

They also failed to grasp that empowerment is finally a greedy principle. When tweens talk about girl power on websites and in interviews, they make it clear that pure, undiluted self-esteem tends to ride roughshod over values smelling of self-restraint. "It's about not letting anyone judge you." "It's about no limitations," they write. *YM* magazine for teens has run a section called "Girl Zone: Your Guide to Kicking Butt."

Teachers confirm that, as far as kids are concerned, empowerment amounts to an in-your-face attitude. "If you tell them, 'You have to do your homework, or you won't graduate,'" says a counselor in a Queens middle school, "they look at you and say, 'So?'" A fifth-grade teacher at a tony East Side private girls' school says, "There's a lot of calling out. You try to get them to raise their hands, to wait their turn. They're very impatient and demanding. They challenge every point on the test. They insist on attention immediately." In Hollywood it is said that tweens roar with pleasure when the *Titanic* character played by Kate Winslet tells her mother to shut up and punctuates her order with an obscene gesture.

Of course, girls are not the only beneficiaries of the ideology of child empowerment. Boys also are enjoying the reign of "no limitations." Faced with students who have been taught the lessons of their own empowerment and who have no experience of authoritative, limit-setting adults at home, educators find themselves coping with a growing indifference toward authority. It's a situation the schools have trouble handling. When they want to discipline boys who are caught writing obscenities in a girl's yearbook, or stuffing a backpack down the toilet, or throwing a stink bomb in the school auditorium—to cite a few of the examples I heard—school officials are not likely to receive any support from the parent. Seeing their job as being their child's advocate in the narrowest, legalistic sense, parents of the culprits in these instances cajoled, manipulated, and argued against any attempt by the school to have their sons face the music.

It is likely that girls' traditional role as goody-goodies used to act as a brake on boys' natural tendency toward restlessness and machismo. Now, as girls are "empowered" to become as bad as they wanna be, boys are "empowered" to become even badder. "Sixth-graders used to be benign and afraid of adults," Bedford, New York, principal Jim Alloy told me. "Now you see some of them who are so defiant, their parents have no idea what to do with them. I have several students from affluent homes with PINS petitions against them." (PINS, which stands for Person in Need of Supervision, allows local authorities to intercede with out-of-control kids.) Whether boy or girl, empowered children, it seems, find support for—or at least, indifference toward—their worst impulses.

Thus tweens, far from being simply a marketing niche group, speak to the very essence of our future. They are the vanguard of a new, decultured generation, isolated from family and neighborhood, shrugged at by parents, dominated by peers, and delivered into the hands of a sexualized and status- and fad-crazed marketplace.

A second-grade teacher told me that, at her school's yearly dance festival, she is finding it increasingly difficult to interest her seven-year-olds in traditional kid stuff like the Mexican hat dance or the hokey-pokey. They want to dress up like the Spice Girls and shimmy away. Look for the tweening of America to continue its downward march.

[1998]

WHAT'S WRONG WITH THE KIDS

Nine months ago, two seemingly ordinary boys from normal middle-class families walked into their high school in an affluent suburb of Denver and shot and killed twelve of their classmates and a teacher before finally turning their guns on themselves. It was a watershed moment in contemporary American life, a definitive fall from innocence that made parents and teachers look on their kids with unfamiliar feelings of anxiety and doubt. There had been other school shootings, of course. But Columbine—the name itself quickly settled into the lexicon—tapped far more deeply into a lurking fear that even during these unprecedentedly good times something might be going wrong with the nation's kids.

What troubled Americans about Columbine was the combination of the extraordinarily willful viciousness of the massacre and the very ordinary middle-classness of its perpetrators and its setting. One could explain violence in inner-city schools: poverty and urban crime had been intertwined since the days of Dickens's London. And, though no one might say it out loud, many Americans could pass over a school shooting in Jonesboro, Arkansas, or West Paducah, Kentucky, without too much comment. The folk in the hills and hollers, Mark Twain taught the nation, can sometimes be a little irrational.

But Columbine was different. Columbine made us wonder if we had been in denial about some sickness at the heart of the middle-class culture that most American kids know as reality. "Where were the parents?" many people asked, bewildered at how two teenagers could build up an arsenal in their own bedrooms without their mother or father knowing. "What kind of schools have we created?" others wondered, on hearing that the two were making videos and writing essays for school about their vile fantasies without anyone being particularly impressed.

This fall, stories from two unlikely (because relentlessly conventional) sources, PBS's "Frontline" and *Time* magazine, began to give us an answer to these questions. By entering deeply into the daily lives of American middle-class children as they interact with their families and schools, the stories offer some real insight into the roots of the teen alienation and emptiness that culminated in Columbine. They add up to a devastating portrait of adults who were not neglectful or abusive in any conventional sense but who, apart from lavish houses and abundant entertainment, have nothing of substance to pass on to children. Without the producers and writers fully understanding what they have uncovered, their portrait reinforces the suspicion that Columbine may reflect a spiritual and emotional void within contemporary American middle-class culture, into which troubled teenagers can easily pour their most grotesque and often rage-filled fantasies.

The adults who appear in the first and most important of these portraits, "The Lost Children of Rockdale County," which aired on the PBS series "Frontline," in October, would seem to have everything to offer children. About twenty-five miles east of Atlanta, Rockdale is Littleton's sociological twin, a booming, affluent suburb—"the fastest-growing settlement in human history," according to some locals quoted on the show. As is the case with Littleton, many Rockdale residents are newcomers to the region who have succeeded in their search for the good life. We get innumerable images of the wide streets of pristine subdivisions and newly sprouted McMansions, with their cathedral ceilings and airy, granite-countered kitchens. And, in fact, the mothers and fathers who inhabit these perfect houses do a good deal of what we hear good parents today ought to do: they coach Little League teams, they go on family vacations, they fix dinner for the kids. In the end, though, they remain utterly clueless when it comes to turning their mansions into homes where children can learn how to lead meaningful lives. Devoid of strong beliefs, seemingly bereft of meaningful experience to pass on to their young, they have at their center a vague emptiness that comes to seem the exact inverse of the meticulous opulence of their homes. The "Frontline" episode could just have easily been titled "The Lost Adults of Rockdale County."

The occasion for the show was an outbreak of syphilis that ultimately led health officials to treat two hundred teenagers. What was so remarkable was not that two hundred teenagers in a large suburban area were having sex and had overlapping partners. It was the way they were having sex. This was teen sex as *Lord of the Flies* author William Golding might have imagined it, a heart-of-darkness tribal rite of such degradation that it makes a collegiate "hookup" look like splendor in the grass. Group sex was commonplace, as were thirteen-year-old participants. Kids would watch the Playboy cable TV channel and make a game of imitating everything they saw. They tried almost every permutation of sexual activity imaginable—vaginal, oral, anal, girl on girl, several boys with a single girl, or several girls with a boy. (The only taboo was homosexual activity among boys.) During some drunken parties, one girl might be "passed around" in a game. A number of the kids had upward of fifty partners. Some kids engaged in what they called a "sandwich"—while a girl performs oral sex on one boy, she is penetrated vaginally by another boy and anally by yet another.

According to the producers, it was the profound loneliness of these children that led them to seek a "surrogate family" in the company of their peers. No one could dispute that these children are lonely. Some are the virtual orphans of broken and dysfunctional homes. Others were simply the children of part-time parents, who were out of the house working long hours to provide their children with lavish homes, cars, cell phones, and the latest teen fashions. Most of the sex parties took place after school, between 3:00 p.m. and 7:00 p.m., in houses emptied of working adults. Other times, kids slipped out of the house after midnight, without waking their exhausted parents.

But it gradually becomes clear that the absence in these kids' lives is not limited to office hours, and the loneliness they suffer goes beyond being left alone. Their parents, even when at home, seem disconnected. As the producers see it, one of the problems is that these families spend most of their time, including meals, in front of the television. "You just go fix your plate, eat, watch TV, finish watchin' whatever you're watchin'," one girl explains. The camera follows a boy named Kevin as he shuffles from the kitchen (with television, of course) out to his bedroom in the family pool house, where he has, inexplicably, two televisions, both enormous, and both flickering at the time of his interviews. In fact, the television is on in the background during a number of the show's home interviews, a detail that turns out to be more than local color. A Kaiser Foundation study released shortly after the "The Lost Children of Rockdale County" aired found that two-thirds of children have televisions in their rooms and that 58 percent of parents admitted that the TV was on during dinner.

Yet, surely a diet of "The Simpsons" and "Dawson's Creek" is more a symptom than a cause of middle-class ills. The truth is, though the show's creators can't quite put their finger on the problem, these shadowy adults have removed themselves from the universal task of parenthood: that is, guiding and shaping the young. And they have done so not because they are too busy at work or watching television but because they have no cultural tools with which to do their job. They know they must love their children; they know they must provide for them—both of which they can do abundantly. The producers are clearly and rightly critical of the way these adults have translated material goods into the sum and substance of parental obligation. But when it comes to the cultural resources that would outfit their children with the moral awareness and worthy aspirations that would help them form a firm sense of self, these parents are deeply impoverished. Here the producers can only make some ineffectual speculation.

Yet the producers' inability to define this scarcity is as important a part of the Rockdale story as the sex parties and syphilis outbreak, for it reflects a more general confusion about the cultural impoverishment suffered by many children today. The profile of one father and daughter in particular dramatizes how the Rockdale parents and the media are similarly befuddled. Amy, a soft-spoken and pallid young woman, who smiles shyly as she tells her story, clearly has had all the benefits of a privileged childhood. We see shots from the family videos and photo albums—doubtless made by parents bursting with pleasure—of the braided girl whacking a ball during a Little League game, grinning sweetly as she carries

her Easter basket in her pretty party dress, and nestling happily in the lap of her contentedly smiling father. In fact, Amy's
father did everything the books tell you to do. (Amy's mother
refused to be interviewed.) He coached her baseball team; the
family went on vacations together; he appears to have good
reason to say, "We were close." But—he finally admits, in
what appears to be a moment of revelation—they watched
too much television. "We've got TVs in every room in the
house," he says. "I watch my programs. My wife watches her
programs. . . . Much of the time we had together was not together." Pressed, he says forlornly, "I guess we should have
talked more."

Can this really explain how this spunky, beloved little girl
became a teenager so desperately lonely that, urged on by two
boys, she engaged in rough sex in front of her terrified three-
year-old nephew and that she allowed herself to be used as a
ferry service by "friends" whom she sensed liked her only
"because I had a car"? It seems we are to believe so. During
another scene, a health expert tells, with heartfelt frustration
we are evidently supposed to share, about the reaction of the
families of Rockdale when she speaks at a public meeting
about the syphilis epidemic. A minister had turned to her and
exclaimed about the parents: "Don't they see? Don't they see
it's them? They don't talk to their children!" This insight is
certainly consistent with prevailing expert wisdom. The
Kaiser Foundation, in conjunction with Children Now, for instance, has begun a campaign entitled "Talking with Kids
About Tough Issues," which implies that the problem facing
adults today is that they are failing "to impart their own values and, most importantly, to create an atmosphere of open
communication with their children on any issue."

But while it goes without saying that parents should talk
to their children and "impart their own values"—is there any-

one who believes they shouldn't?—this advice begs the obvious question: What exactly is it they are supposed to say? What values are they supposed to impart? To this question, no one—neither the Kaiser Foundation nor the "Frontline" producers—dares venture an answer. Should they tell their children it's not a good idea for them to be having sex with forty partners? Why not? Because they might get syphilis, or because it violates all sense of dignity and modesty? Should they recommend their child see a therapist? A minister? A gynecologist? An expert on Tantric sex? It doesn't seem to matter, as long as they're talking and expressing their "values." Talking and imparting values show that adults are "caring."

Yet the "Frontline" producers unwittingly lead us to the conclusion that adults are not talking to their children for the same reason experts themselves can only deliver these platitudes. They don't believe there are any firm values to impart. These parents undoubtedly do not approve of group sex or sexually transmitted diseases or, for that matter, shooting one's classmates. But they have absorbed from the surrounding culture an ethos of nonjudgmentalism, which has drained their beliefs on these matters of all feeling and force. This suspension of all conviction helps explain the bland, sad air of many of these interviews. "They have to make decisions, whether to take drugs, to have sex," the mother of Kevin, the boy who lives in the pool house, intones expressionlessly. "I can give them my opinion, tell them how I feel. But they have to decide for themselves." It's hard to see how imparting her values will do anything to help her child. After all, these values have no gravity or truth. They are only her opinion.

The children of Rockdale know full well that their parents have nothing to say to them. "In my family, you do what you want to do. No one is going to stop you," Kevin says factually, without a hint of rebellion or arrogance. True, his mother did at one time attempt to be a parent to Kevin's older sister but gave up, because she found "it was easier to let her [do what she wanted]. We got along better." Convinced that there are no values worth fighting for, the lost adults of Rockdale County have abdicated the age-old distinction between parents and children and have settled for being their children's friends and housemates. "We're pretty much like best friends or something," one girl said of her parents. "I mean, I can pretty much tell 'em how I feel, what I wanna do, and they'll let me do it." "I don't really consider her a mom all that much," another girl agrees about her own mother. "She takes care of me and such, but I consider her a friend more."

When adults turn into friends, childhood must disappear. Childhood cannot exist with no adults around. The children of Rockdale, still baby-faced and restlessly energetic, have lost all the sense of wonder, spontaneity, and idealism that we ordinarily associate with childhood. One of the most memorable images from the documentary is of three cherubic fourteen-year-olds demonstrating their sexual activities with the stuffed animals that still lie heaped on the bed in one of their rooms. It is in this child's bedroom, whose walls are decorated with graffiti, some of it obscene, that they also chant the lyrics of their favorite rap song: "He can get the bitch fucked, but how many can get the dick sucked," goes one of the lines. The tone of their delivery is a mixture of robotic chanting and giggling, and it captures perfectly the pathetic struggle inside them between the nihilism their own degraded experience has taught them and the childishness that nature insists still defines them.

For nihilism, as Columbine seems to have taught us, is the eventual outcome for that considerable number of children today who are growing up deprived of any inherited wisdom about the longings and limits of human nature. Left to feel their way through life by themselves, they will inevitably stumble into experiences against which they have no defenses, experiences that will ultimately leave them numb. One thinks of Heather, who by the time she was twelve was left by her single mother to fend for herself for a week at a time when the mother was away on business trips. The child turned to alcohol and drugs and one day woke up to realize she had been raped while she was passed out. Her own words offer a sad epigraph on the weightless life to which she was abandoned. "The first time that you have sex, you think it's 'cause it means something," she says at fourteen. "But then you realize it doesn't. You just don't really care anymore."

Among her peers, even the reality of a serious disease becomes nothing to get excited about. Taking her daughter to the county health office to be tested for syphilis, one mother assumed the girl would be chastened. Not at all. The kids laughed and gave each other the high-five. "We thought it was funny," one girl said of the occasion. "'Oooh, you got syphilis,' you know. . . . It was like the cooties game little kids play, you know." These children's deadened sensibilities leave them incapable of horror—and, for all their sexual adventures, of pleasure. "Sex sucks, actually," says another. "I think sex was made for guys, because you just lay there, and you're just like, 'Get off me, what are you doing?'"

A month to the day after Columbine, Rockdale County was the scene of another school shooting, when a fifteen-year-old sophomore opened fire and wounded six people at Heritage High School, where some of the kids interviewed for "Frontline" were enrolled. T. J. Solomon, the boy who committed the crime, was said to be depressed. After watching "The Lost Children of Rockdale County," one can begin to understand why.

Of course, it would be oversimplifying things to blame

parents for the ills of children like those of Rockdale and leave it at that. Parents are not some subculture with its own belief-system and habits; they are citizens of a wider culture, and in their child-rearing practices they are conforming to its demands. An October cover story in *Time*, entitled "A Week in the Life of a High School: What It's Really Like Since Columbine," illustrates that culture at work inside our educational institutions. *Time* chose to base its diary on Webster Groves High School in Webster Groves, Missouri—a town of about 23,000, ten miles southwest of St. Louis—precisely because it struck them as so ordinary. (In fact, CBS chose Webster Groves to be the subject of a 1966 documentary for the same reason.) Indeed, as in Littleton and Rockdale, it is the ordinariness of Webster Groves that makes its story so troubling.

Like the lost adults of Rockdale County, Webster Groves's educators have also disengaged themselves from the task of shaping and training the young. And like Rockdale parents, they view the cultural heritage that might transform these youngsters into morally aware, aesthetically and intellectually alert adults as optional, a matter of opinion rather than of firmly held conviction. Thus the few ambitious college-bound students of Webster Groves may choose to read serious literature and do serious math. However, those who don't feel like it—that is, the large majority—can choose to remain in their complacent, uncultivated state. The effect is to turn the institution into day care for teenagers, a high school baby-sitting service to keep kids off the streets. Students can satisfy the most challenging requirement, English (or "communication skills," as the school gratingly calls it), for instance, by taking journalism courses or a children's literature class, in which they read books by Dr. Seuss and other works written at the third-grade level or below. Or they might take a dumbed-down tenth-grade English class. On the day the *Time* writers visited, this class was analyzing a short story called "Sweet Potato Pie." The teacher describes eating sweet potato pie, ham hocks, collard greens. "And what do all these things have in common?" the teacher challenges her group of fifteen-year-old students. "They don't care if you learn," says one junior boy astutely. "They only care if you pass."

It could be argued that, unlike the parents of Rockdale County, Webster Groves educators have a good excuse for their surrender. State officials have made it clear that they view teaching students as secondary to educators' central task: to keep kids from dropping out and becoming social menaces. The state of Missouri gives bonus money to schools that have been able to reduce their dropout rate, and in Webster Groves that has amounted to $150,000, an irresistible sum considering that the school is staring at a $1.2 million deficit. Yet these funds also turn out to give students a way to black-mail teachers. Not only does the attendance bonus force teachers to dumb down the curriculum—"you promise not to ask us to read anything above a sixth-grade level, and we'll promise to stay in school" is the unspoken bargain—it also renders them powerless to enforce discipline against all but the most threatening infractions. Students can curse at teachers and saunter in late to class without penalty; teachers know the administration can't do much to back them up.

Most of the faculty has also stopped assigning more than fifteen minutes of homework a night. One teacher estimates that only 15 percent of her class does the work she assigns, and kids report doing ten minutes, thirty minutes a night, tops. ("They're safe here, and they can learn in class, even if they aren't doing homework," an assistant principal explains.) And teachers assign little homework, so that kids have plenty of time to do what they really want to do: make money. Students commonly work thirty or even forty hours a week in bagel or video stores—not to save up for college but to buy the $400 leather jackets and cool cars whose central importance in life their education does nothing to challenge.

In Webster Groves, as in Rockdale, adults who have surrendered any semblance of the authority that normally invests those of greater experience and understanding try to disguise their negligence by pretending they are their charges' friends and peers. The *Time* article opens when the principal arrives for a predawn workout in a Goofy T-shirt, and her garb sets the tone of much that follows. Two teachers frequently engage in practical jokes, such as shooting Super Soaker water guns at students from the roof, a prank that led a frightened neighbor who could only see their outlines to call the police. The week that *Time* visited the school, the two climbed up to the school roof again, this time to dangle the head of a female mannequin they'd named Headrietta so that it hangs in front of a classroom window and elicits the screams of female students. Comments *Time* about one of the zany pair: "It's hard to tell whether Yates, physics and astronomy teacher and chair of the science department, is a member of the faculty or still a kid." Yates's strenuous efforts to keep things friendly don't always work. His students continue to "dis" him or call him "asshole," behavior that Yates reassures himself is a sign that they are "comfortable" with him.

Extreme as it is, Yates's evasion is the way many adults today tell themselves that they are doing well by the young. As long as the kids stay in school, as long as their self-esteem is unthreatened, as long as the adult-child friendship appears relatively trouble-free, they can tell themselves they have a "good relationship with the kids." Indeed, the writers of "A Week in the Life" depict the educators of Webster Groves as caring adults who put in extra time going to school football games and playing in faculty-student softball competitions, as well as reaching out to a teen whose mother just died or another whose parents are getting divorced.

But none of this can fill the void left by their own failure, and doubtless that of most of their students' parents, to represent a coherent moral and intellectual order. One of the main jobs of the educators of Webster Groves is to manage the decline brought about by their own abdication. Though the school has no guards or metal detectors, the principal and her assistants, including a detective, wander the halls between classes with walkie-talkies. Officials installed costly tracer equipment on the school telephone after a bomb scare last year. The faculty has crisis-management seminars for working out responses to hypothetical emergencies. The school keeps a wary eye on the many kids on medication, and teachers are on the alert for those who suddenly lose interest in activities or whose grades decline.

Erik Erikson once defined adulthood as a period of generativity, when the mature nurture the vulnerable young and prepare them for independent life. What the stories from both "Frontline" and *Time* suggest is that in many parts of America adulthood in this sense has vanished. Adults have no meaningful cultural nourishment for filling the empty imaginations of their children, nothing to give order to their chaotic, unformed selves. For middle-class kids, a generation richer than any in human history, the predicament is grim. Setting out on the search for human meaning, they see adults staring vacantly at the ground.

It's enough to make some of them pretty mad.

[2000]

THE TEEN MOMMY TRACK

Fourteen-year-old Taisha Brown is thinking of having a baby. She doesn't say so directly, and it doesn't seem about to happen tomorrow, but she smiles coyly at the question. Around her way—a housing project in the South Bronx—lots of girls have babies. Her sixteen-year-old cousin just gave birth a few months ago, and she enjoys helping with the infant. "I love babies," the braided, long-legged youngster says sweetly. "They're so cute. My mother already told me, 'If you get pregnant, you won't have an abortion. You'll have the baby, and your grandmother and I will help out.'" What about school or making sure the baby has a father? "I want to be a lawyer . . . or maybe a teacher. Why do I need to worry about a father? My mother raised me and my sister just fine without one."

Taisha Brown seems likely to become one of the nearly half-million teenagers who give birth each year in the United States, a number that gives the nation the dubious honor of the highest teen birth rate in the developed world. About two-thirds of those girls are unmarried; many are poor. Americans debating welfare reform and the state of the family have no shortage of opinions about the cause of the problem: welfare dependency, low self-esteem, economic decline, ignorance about birth control—the list could go on and on. All these theories fail to explain the actual experiences of teenagers, because they ignore the psychology of adolescence, the differences between underclass and mainstream cultural norms, and the pivotal role of family structure in shaping young people's values and expectations.

To get a clearer focus on the teen pregnancy problem, I spoke with some thirty new or expectant young mothers and sometimes with their boyfriends, nurses, teachers, and social workers. (To protect their privacy, I've identified the teenagers with fictitious names.) I asked about their lives, their expectations, and their babies. The girls' stories vary widely: from a fifteen-year-old, forced to live in seven different foster homes over the last five years, whose sunken eyes hint of Blakean misery, to a seventeen-year-old college student who describes herself as "old-fashioned" and has been cheerfully dating the same boy for five years.

It gradually became clear that, however separated they may be by degrees of poverty and family disorder, these girls all live in a similar world: a culture—or subculture, to be precise—with its own values, beliefs, sexual mores, and, to a certain extent, its own economy. It is, by and large, a culture created and ruled by children, a never-never land almost completely abandoned by fathers and, in some sad cases, by mothers as well. But if such a culture is made possible by adult negligence, it is also enabled by mixed messages coming from parents, teachers, social workers, and the media—from mainstream society itself.

Sociologists sometimes use the term "life script" to refer to the sense individuals have of the timing and progression of the major events in their lives. At an early age we internalize our life script as it is modeled for us by our family and community. The typical middle-class American script is familiar to most readers: childhood, a protracted period of adolescence and young adulthood required for training in a complex society, beginning of work, and, only then, marriage and child-bearing. The assumption is not merely that young adults should be financially self-supporting before they have children. It is also that they must achieve a degree of maturity by putting the storms of adolescence well behind them before taking on the demanding responsibility of molding their own children's identity.

But for the minority teens I spoke with, isolated as they are from mainstream mores, this script is unrecognizable. With little adult involvement in young people's daily activities and decisions, their adolescence takes on a different form. It is less a stormy but necessary continuation of childhood—a time of emotional, social, and intellectual development—than a quasi-adulthood. The mainstream rites of maturity—college, first apartment, first serious job—hold little emotional meaning for these youngsters. Many of the girls I spoke with say they aspire to a career, but these ambitions do not appear to arise out of any deep need to place themselves in the world. Few dream of living on their own. And all view marriage as irrelevant, vestigial.

To these girls and young women, the only thing that symbolizes maturity is a baby. A pregnant fourteen-year-old may refer to herself as a "woman" and her boyfriend as her "husband." Someone who waits until thirty or even twenty-five to have her first child seems a little weird, like the spinster aunt of yesteryear. "I don't want to wait to have a baby until I'm old," one seventeen-year-old Latino boy told me. "At thirty, I run around with him, I have a heart attack."

The teen mommy track has the tacit support of elders like Taisha's mother, many of whom themselves gave birth as teenagers. Even if they felt otherwise, the fact is that single mothers in the inner city don't expect to have much control over their kids, especially their sons, after age thirteen—on any matter. And, with few exceptions, the fathers of the kids I spoke with were at best a ghostly presence in their lives.

Commonly, mothers expect their older children to care for, and to socialize, younger siblings and cousins, a process that, as Ronald L. Taylor of the University of Connecticut speculates, disconnects children from adult control. Fifteen-year-old Rosie, now carrying a child of her own, describes how she had always taken care of her younger brothers, though their mother did not work outside the home. The youngsters started calling their sister "Mom" when she was nine. In a heartrending example of this phenomenon, Leon Dash, in his book *When Children Want Children*, tells of a baby-sitting six-year-old girl hysterically trying to figure out how to mix formula for her infant brother.

Most adolescents are heartbreaking conformists, but kids with little parental supervision are especially vulnerable to their friends' definitions of status and style. As Greg Donaldson, author of *The Ville*, notes, the streets and projects of the inner city are dominated by kids; one sees few middle-aged or elderly adults. It's no wonder such children look to their peers from an early age for guidance and emotional sustenance. *Harper's* magazine quoted a pregnant fourteen-year-old, who had been taught about birth control, abortion, and the trials of single motherhood, and who captures the spirit of this teen world I saw so often: "All my friends have babies. I was beginning to wonder what was wrong with me that I didn't have one too."

In this never-never land, having a baby is a role-playing adventure. In the labor room, nurses say, younger teens sometimes suck their thumbs or grasp their favorite stuffed animal between contractions. The young mother's boyfriend, if he is still around, plays "husband"; the new baby is a doll that mothers love to dress up and take out for walks in shiny new strollers. In one high school program to discourage pregnancy, I was told, each girl had to carry around a five-pound bag of rice for a week, always keeping it in sight or paying someone to watch it. By the end of the week, several girls had dressed up their bags in clothes from Baby Gap. "It's like a fashion show," says one expectant eighteen-year-old. "At least for the first two years. Then they're not so cute anymore. After that, the kids are dressed like bums."

While the girls play mother, some of the lost boys of never-never land seek sexual adventure to test their early manhood. They often brag about their conquests, which they achieve with promises—sneakers, clothes, a ride in a nice car—and with flattery. "You know I love you, baby," they'll tell a girl. "You're so pretty." Fathering children is also a sign of manhood. A group of four disgruntled young Hispanic girls, strolling their babies down a shopping street in Brooklyn, say they have sworn off men forever and that they know of boys who get tattooed with their children's names like bombardiers tallying hits on the sides of their airplanes. Legend among these girls has it that the occasional adventurer surreptitiously punctures a condom to outwit his reluctant conquest.

But bravado, playacting, and fashion-consciousness are not the whole story, particularly for the older adolescents I met. For many of them, a baby stirs up a love they imagine will bring meaning to their drifting lives; it becomes an object of romance that beckons them away from the cynical, often brutal world in which they live. Frank, a seventeen-year-old African-American father, waxes joyful over his six-month-old daughter, who came as a sign that he must put away childish things. "Babies don't walk, they don't talk, but they get inside you so fast. Before she was born, I was a Casanova. I didn't even know who I was with. I was hanging out all the time, doing wild things. The baby slowed me down, put the brakes on things, and made me think about my future." According to University of Pennsylvania sociologist Elijah Anderson, some mothers actually want their teenage sons to have children in the hopes that they will settle down.

The early sexual activity of these unsupervised young-sters—it's not uncommon to hear of experienced eleven- and twelve-year-olds—is old news by now. Rape and abuse help fuel this precocity; some estimates claim that more than 60 percent of teen mothers have been victims, with stepfathers or mothers' boyfriends often implicated. But early sex is also part of the accepted mores of teens on the underclass mommy track. Christie, a sixteen-year-old Latino whose tidy ponytail, shorts, white socks, and sneakers might lead one to look for a tennis racket rather than the month-old daughter she held in her arms, explained that she had her first sexual encounter two years earlier because she "was sick of being the only four-teen-year-old virgin around. I didn't really like the guy that much; I was just trying to get my friends off my back. When he started telling people, 'Oh, I had her,' I was really mad. I told everyone, 'No, I was using him.'"

Teenagers, as many can miserably recall from high school, rely on derisive name-calling to enforce conformity to their so-cial codes. Inez, a tough, outspoken twenty-year-old from a Washington Heights Dominican family, describes how her un-conventional behavior was criticized in much the same way a black high achiever is accused of "acting white": "My sister and I are the only ones in my building who don't have babies. When I was younger, kids used to call me names. I never brought a boyfriend around, so they called me a lesbian. They told me I was conceited, that I thought I was better than every-one else, called me 'Miss Virgin.' I tried to stay off the streets." Elijah Anderson found that African-American boys reinforce the value of sex without emotional commitment by ridiculing those who look too enchanted as "househusbands" or "pussy whipped."

Marriage, as far as these kids are concerned, is gone, dead, an unword. Some observers, following William Julius Wilson, have suggested that this is because impoverished men with limited job prospects don't make likely husbands. But to listen to the kids themselves is to hear another theme—a mistrust of the opposite sex so profound that the ancient war between the sexes seems to have turned into Armageddon. Rap singers describe girls as "ho's" (whores) or "bitches," but even some of the more modest individuals I spoke with see them as tricky Calypsos scheming to entrap boys—a view sometimes reinforced by a boy's own husbandless mother. The thirty-five-year-old mother of an eighteen-year-old explains that she wants him "to have his fun. I don't care who he's sleeping with. I just don't want him to be trapped." For their part, girls see boys as either feckless braggarts and mama's boys or bossy intruders. "You're cursin' at me!" mocks Stephanie, an African American from the Bronx, when I asked her if she thought of marrying her boyfriend of two years, father of a child due this summer. "Why would I want to have some man askin' me, 'Where you goin'; what you doin'?'"

Seventeen-year-old Roberto speaks woodenly throughout our conversation as he stands dutifully next to his expectant girlfriend, who is waiting to be seen by a nurse at Methodist Hospital in Brooklyn. But when I ask if he wants to get married, it is as if I have applied an electric shock. His eyebrows shoot upward and his mouth drops. "Married? Not until I'm thirty-five or thirty at least. You get married, the trouble starts. Marriage is a big commitment." But isn't a child an even bigger commitment? Evidently not. "A baby is from the heart. Marriage is a piece of paper, it's official. I'll be responsible for my child, make sure I support him and visit him, but marriage. . . ." He shakes his head.

Stephanie plans to train to be an optician while leaving her child in the care of her mother—who, like many of these grandmothers still in their thirties, quickly shifted from anger over her daughter's pregnancy to delight over the imminent arrival of what she now calls "my baby." Like most of her sisters, when asked if she worries that a baby will get in the way of her plans, Stephanie answers emphatically, "No! Not at all!"

Nurses say they hear girls dreaming of "having their own budget" courtesy of welfare. But of all the new or expectant mothers I spoke with, only one shrugged when I asked if she had any thoughts about what kind of work she might do. About their economic futures, most girls seemed more unrealistic than demoralized or lazy. With no parents watching over them and cracking the educational whip, and with little intellectual drive or ability to organize their adolescent urges, their career notions seem hopelessly dreamy. Several said they wanted to be a lawyer or an obstetrician the way a four-year-old, asked what he wants to be when he grows up, answers he wants to be an astronaut.

Teenage dreaminess unchecked by adult common sense defines never-never land as much as conformity and bravado do. Lorraine Barton, a pediatric nurse at Methodist Hospital, describes a progression noted by many others in the field: "A lot of kids, and I mean boys and girls, are thrilled with having a baby. They love to dress them up and show them off; they like the baby carriages and all that stuff. But they don't seem to understand the baby will grow up. Around the time the baby begins to move around and be a separate person trying to go his own way, they lose interest. These are kids themselves, but they haven't had a chance to act like that. You can be sure they don't want to be chasing a toddler. It's also around this time that you see a lot of relationships end. The boys come around to visit, bring some Pampers, and later take the child for ice cream. But that's it." Even Frank, the chastened father of a six-month-old, says of his child: "I at least want to have a relationship with her. I want to know what's going on in her life." How could he envision anything more? He barely knows his own father.

The failure to understand the power of cultural norms over youngsters, especially norms that coincide so neatly with biological urges, has created a policy world that parallels but never quite touches the never-never land of underclass teenagers. Dwellers in the policy world seem unable to make the leap of sympathetic imagination needed to understand the mindset of the underclass adolescent. Instead they assume that everyone is born internally programmed to follow the middle-class life script. If you don't follow the mainstream script, it's not because you don't have it there inside you but because something has gotten in your way and derailed you—poverty, say, or low self-esteem, or lack of instruction in some technique such as birth control.

According to this view, to say that teen pregnancy perpetuates poverty has it backward. Instead, writes Katha Pollit in *The Nation*, "It would be closer to the truth to say that poverty causes early and unplanned childbearing. . . . Girls with bright futures—college, jobs, travel—have abortions. It's the girls who have nothing to postpone who become mothers." But evidence contradicts the notion that early childbearing is an automatic response to poverty and dim futures. After all, birthrates of women aged fifteen to nineteen reached their lowest point this century during the hard times of the depression. And in the past forty years, while the U.S. economy has risen and fallen, out-of-wedlock teen births have only gone in one direction—up, and steeply. Meanwhile, in rural states like Maine, Montana, and Idaho, the out-of-wedlock birthrate among African Americans is low, not because there is less poverty but because traditional, mainstream norms hold sway.

A related but also flawed theory is that a lack of self-esteem caused by poverty and neglect is at the root of early pregnancy. But the responses of the girls I spoke with were characterized more by a naive adolescent optimism than by a sad humility, depression, or hopelessness. Indeed, a study commissioned by the American Association of University Women found that the group with the highest self-esteem is African-American boys, followed closely by African-American girls.

Self-esteem has a different foundation in a subculture that, unlike elite culture, values motherhood over career achievement. To listen to some policymakers, one might think that wanting to become a lawyer or an anchorwoman—and possessing the requisite orderliness, discipline, foresight, and bourgeois willingness to delay gratification—are natural instincts rather than traits developed over time through adults' prodding and example. With little sympathetic understanding of the underclass teen heart, David Ellwood, an assistant secretary of Health and Human Services, has written: "The overwhelming proportion of teenagers do not want children, and those who do simply cannot realize what they are in for. It is not rational to get pregnant at 17, no matter what the alternatives appear to be."

Ellwood's notion of rationality presupposes that a teenager is following the middle-class life script. This failure to understand the underclass teen's worldview leads him to embrace another deep-seated but mistaken theory: that unwed teen childbearing is the result of inadequate sex education. "Teenage pregnancy is a matter of information, contraception, and sexual activity, all of which might plausibly be changed," he writes. Most sex education curriculums, including those that "stress abstinence," rely on the same belief in a fundamentally rational teenager. They set out to train students in "decision-making skills," "planning skills," or something mysteriously called "life skills." Explain the facts, detail the process, the bulb will go on, and the kids will get their condoms ready or just say no.

These approaches are not so much wrong as irrelevant, for they ignore the qualities of mind that are a prerequisite for developing complex skills. Christie told a story whose general outline I heard more than once. "I was on birth-control pills. But then I slept at my cousin's house and missed a day. I took two pills the next day. I guess that happened a few times. The nurse had told me I had to take them every day, but I couldn't." Birth control, Christie unwittingly reminds us, requires organization, foresight, and self-control, often at precisely those moments when passions are most insistent. These are qualities that even adolescents from privileged backgrounds, much less those untutored in the ways of bourgeois self-denial, are often still in the process of developing. Something far deeper than simple ignorance or lack of technical skill is at work here.

Governor Mario Cuomo took the fallacy of the underclass teenager with a bourgeois soul to its logical extreme when he remarked recently: "If you took a fifteen-year-old with a child, but put her in a clean apartment, got her a diploma, gave her the hope of a job . . . that would change everything." But it takes more than a governor's decree to transform an underclass fifteen-year-old into a middle-class adult. Many programs for teen mothers find it necessary to teach them not only how to interview for a job but also how to shop for food, how to budget money, how to plan a menu, even how to brush their teeth. Programs like these point to the devilishly tricky problem of resolving the tension between the mainstream and underclass life scripts.

Moreover, instead of discouraging unwed teen pregnancy, such programs often end up smoothing it into an alternative life-style. If Taisha Brown does become pregnant, she will be able to leave her dull, impersonal school for a homey, nurturing middle school for pregnant girls like herself. Later she will very likely find a high school with a nursery where she can stop by between classes and visit with her baby, attend parenting classes, receive advice about public assistance, and share experiences with other teen mothers in counseling groups. Kathleen Sylvester of the Progressive Policy Institute, who has visited such a school in Baltimore, says it is far nicer than ordinary public schools. "It's cheerful, warm; you get hugs and lots of attention." These programs have been introduced with the best of intentions—to ensure that teen mothers will continue their education. But because of them, it will seem to Taisha that the world around her fully endorses early motherhood.

Conservatives, most notably Charles Murray, see the roots of this normalization in Aid to Families with Dependent Children and other welfare subsidies that provide an economic incentive for illegitimacy. But even if welfare ignited the initial explosion of out-of-wedlock births in the 1960s, its role in shaping social norms today seems less vital. The Census Bureau reports that the number of children living with a never-married parent soared by more than 70 percent between 1983 and 1993. The birthrate among single women in professional and managerial jobs tripled during the same period. Increasingly America seems a land in which, as Mort Sahl has joked, the only people who want to get married are a few Catholic priests, and the only people who want to have babies are lawyers nearing menopause—and impoverished children. In a world so out of whack, welfare seems only a bit player.

All of the prevailing analyses of teen childbearing, both liberal and conservative, neglect a troubling truth apparent throughout most of human history: nothing could be more natural than a sixteen-year-old having a baby. But in complex societies such as our own, which require not just more schooling but what the great German sociologist Norbert Elias calls a longer "civilizing process," the sixteen-year-old, though physically mature, is considered an adolescent, a late-stage child, unready for parenthood. This quasi-childhood constitutes a fragile limbo between physical maturation and social or technical competence, between puberty and childbearing, one that requires careful ordering of insistent, awakening sexual urges. This century's gallery of juvenile delinquents, gangs, hippies, and teen parents should remind us of the difficulty of this project. Even now, social workers report seeing fourteen- and fifteen-year-old wives from immigrant Albanian and Yugoslavian families coming to pregnancy clinics. The truth is that adolescent childbearing was commonplace even in the staid 1950s, when a quarter of all American women had babies before the age of twenty, though of course almost always within wedlock.

But two related social changes occurred in the late 1960s: early marriage came under suspicion, and the sexual revolution caught fire. This meant that the strategies societies generally use to control the hormonal riot of adolescence—prohibiting sex entirely and encouraging marriage within a few years of puberty—both became less workable. The "shotgun wedding" became a thing of the past. As a result, American adolescence became longer, looser, more hazardous.

Adolescents at the bottom of the socioeconomic ladder were most harshly affected by these changes. Middle-class kids have more adult eyes watching over them during this precarious period. They also have numerous opportunities for sublimation—a useful Freudian term unfortunately banished along with its coiner from current intellectual fashion—of their urges: sports teams, church or temple groups, vacations, and camp, not to mention decent schools. Their poorer counterparts don't get that attention. It's much less likely that someone watches to see whom they're hanging out with or whether they've done their homework. Their teachers and counselors often don't even know their names. And "solutions" like contraceptive giveaways, decision-making-skill classes, and even abstinence training only ratify their precocious independence.

Far better would be programs that recognized and channeled the emotional demands of adolescence—intensive sports teams or drama groups, for instance, which simultaneously engage kids' affections and offer constructive, supervised outlets for their energies. According to some teachers who work closely with pregnant teens, births go up nine months after summer and Christmas vacation—further evidence of adolescents' profound need for structure and direction.

Given that unwed teen childbearing has become the norm for a significant subset of American society, the salient question is not why so many girls are having babies but what prevents some of their peers from following this path. I explored that question with a group of five young black and Latino women in their twenties, all of whom had grown up in neighborhoods where the teen mommy track was common. All were college students or graduates acting as peer AIDS counselors for teens in poor areas of the city. None had children.

All but one grew up with both parents; the other was the product of a strict Catholic education in Aruba. If the meeting hadn't been arranged by the New York City Department of Health, I might have suspected a family values agenda at work.

All of these young women said their parents, in addition to loving them, watched and prodded them. "My father used to come out on the street and call me inside," Jocelyn recalls, laughing. "It was so embarrassing, I just learned to get in there before he came out." Intact families seem to provide the emotional weight needed to ballast the increasingly compelling peer group. Clearly, two parents are vastly better than one at keeping the genie of adolescent pregnancy inside the bottle.

These experiences jibe with both common sense and research. Asians, who have strong families and the lowest divorce rate of any ethnic group (3 percent), also have the lowest teen pregnancy rate (6 percent). In a longitudinal study that may be the only one of its kind, sociologist Frank Furstenberg of the University of Pennsylvania periodically followed the children of teen mothers from birth in the 1960s to as old as twenty-one in 1987. His findings couldn't be more dramatic: kids with close relationships with a residential father or long-term stepfather simply did not follow the teenage mommy track. One out of four of the 253 mostly black Baltimoreans in the study had a baby before age nineteen. But not one who had a good relationship with a live-in father had a baby. A close relationship with a father not living at home did not help; indeed, those children were more likely to have a child before nineteen than those with little or no contact with their fathers.

Some social critics, most forcefully Senator Daniel Patrick Moynihan, have insisted on the profound importance of fathers in the lives of adolescent boys. But for girls a father is just as central. Inez, one of the peer AIDS counselors, says she always bristled on hearing boys boast of their female acquaintances, "I can do her anytime," or, "I had her." Any woman who had grown up in a home with an affectionate and devoted father would be similarly disapproving. Having had a firsthand education of the heart, a girl is far less likely to be swayed by the first boy who attempts to snow her with the compliments she may never have heard from a man: "Baby, you look so good," or, "You know I love you."

The ways of love, it seems, must be learned, not from decision-making or abstinence classes, not from watching soap operas or, heaven forbid, from listening to rap music, but through the lived experience of loving and being loved. Judith S. Musick, a developmental psychologist with the Ounce of Prevention Fund, explains that through her relationship with her father, a girl "acquires her attitudes about men and, most importantly, about herself in relation to them." In other words, a girl growing up with a close father internalizes a sense of love, which sends up warning signals when a boy on the prowl begins to strut near her.

Further, a girl hesitates before replacing the attachment she has to her own father with a new love. I recently watched a girl of about twelve walking down the street with her parents. As she skipped along next to them, busily chattering, she held her father's hand and occasionally rested her head against his arm. The introduction of a serious boyfriend into this family romance is unlikely to come soon. Marian Wright Edelman's aphorism has received wide currency: "The best contraceptive is a real future." It would be more accurate to say, "The best contraceptive is a real father and mother."

If it is true that fatherless girls are far more likely to begin sex early, to fall under the sway of swaggering, unreliable men, to become teen parents, and quite simply to accept single parenthood as a norm, we are faced with a gloomy prophecy: the teen mommy track is likely to become more crowded. Nationwide, 57 percent of black children are living with a never-married mother. In many inner-city schools, like those in Central Harlem where the rate of out-of-wedlock births is 85 percent, kids with two parents are oddballs, a status youngsters don't take kindly to. When Taisha Brown has her baby, that child may eventually repeat Taisha's question: "Why do I need to worry about a father? My mother raised me just fine without one." Indeed, it seems inevitable without a transformation of the culture that gave birth to the teen mommy track.

[1994]

MEN AND WOMEN

FEMINISTS AND
THEIR ENEMIES

Recently the *New York Times* published a book review that surely had jaws dropping on both sides of the cultural divide. Written by Richard Bernstein and headlined "Boys, Not Girls, as Society's Victims," it was an extremely sympathetic treatment of Christina Hoff Sommers's *The War Against Boys,* subtitled, in case anyone might fail to get the message, *How Misguided Feminism Is Harming Our Young Men.*

What was going on here? In the ideological mosh pit that is today's *New York Times,* radical feminist thought has long been all but immune from honest scrutiny, let alone criticism. And Sommers, utterly devastating in her critique of the campaign against male nature, has long been at the top of the radical sisterhood's enemies list.

Was this an aberration or the beginnings of a shift in the *Times'*s policy, a faint crack in the bunker of elite opinion?

Well, let's not go overboard. Understanding the way things unfold at the *New York Times* takes the subtlety of a Kremlinologist, and with heavy-handed sixties enthusiast Pinch Sulzberger in charge, the paper is unlikely to return to its classical liberal roots anytime soon. But it's a funny thing about intellectual fraud: keeping it up over the long term is exhausting and dispiriting. Once honest discussion breaks loose, it can be hard to hold down.

At the very least, such a piece serves to illustrate, by contrast, how woefully short on common decency and common sense the paper's coverage of feminism has generally been. Indeed, of all the orthodoxies the paper has so aggressively promoted over the years, from its casting of single parenthood as a triumph of diversity to its insistence in the face of ready data and common sense that AIDS is everyone's disease, none has enjoyed quite the degree of special handling as the feminists' drive to remake humanity.

Over the years, *Times* readers have so come to take this bias for granted that even the most daring leaps in logic and the grossest disregard of fairness tend to pass unnoticed. Underlying it all has been the pretense that radical feminist groups, notably the National Organization for Women (which at its height had fewer members than there are female subscribers to *Playboy*), actually speak for all women. A quick check of Lexis-Nexis reveals that over the past decade NOW has been cited in 802 articles, while, as a quick contrast, the conservative Independent Women's Forum has been mentioned a mere seven times. (Just as telling is the nature of the IWF references. Three report, falsely, that the IWF spurred Ken Starr to write a friend-of-the-court brief on behalf of Paula Jones, and two others are retractions of that story—which *Times* reporters kept repeating anyway.)

Of course, what matters—at the *Times*, anyway—is that among the small percentage of women whose views NOW actually represents are the overwhelming majority of those who write and edit at the paper itself: women, that is, who are militantly pro-choice and for whom career is an all-consuming priority. Indeed, in its varied permutations, the worldview they represent can now be found in every corner of the paper, evident not merely in the almost uniformly flattering news stories and photos of Hillary Clinton or the seriousness accorded the likes of a Susan Sarandon, but in a sports department that has made a prominently placed photo of a female Little League player an annual rite of spring.

But as these things go, the quintessential *Times* worldview comes across most undisguisedly in the paper's book reviews, for here no one even has to pretend to objectivity.

Hardly surprisingly, the literary efforts of staff feminists tend to receive especially fulsome praise: people like Susan Chira, the *Times*'s deputy foreign editor, who for years covered child-related issues, in which role she systematically promoted day care while failing to cover studies that documented its potentially deleterious effects. When her 1998 autobiographical tome, *A Mother's Place: Choosing Work and Family Without Guilt or Blame*, took the same tack, the *Times*'s critic lauded it as a "splendid book . . . [that] makes an eloquent, well-documented case that motherhood does not require martyrdom."

Then there's Natalie Angier, the Pulitzer Prize–winning *Times* science writer, whose *Woman: An Intimate Geography* got special handling even by the *Times*'s version of standards. One of those who sees all existence through the prism of gender, Angier uses her role as science writer to scour nature endlessly for evidence of female superiority and male inferiority. The *Book Review* editors originally assigned her book to the well-known evolutionary biologist Helen Cronin, but they killed that review after it turned out "too negative"—Cronin later reported she'd found Angier's work "totally idiotic. She uses phrases like 'the vagina as a model for the universe itself.'" No problem. The book was reviewed in the daily *Times* by Stanford professor Marilyn Yalom, author of *A History of the Breast*, who pronounced it "dazzling . . . supported by rigorous scientific underpinnings."

Hardly incidentally, a couple of years earlier, Angier had reviewed Yalom's breast book for the *Book Review*, calling it "a fascinating cultural, political and artistic history of our most symbolically freighted body part."

On the other hand, women authors who challenge cherished feminist truths—and, worse, who call women to account for problems ascribed to the bugaboo of patriarchy—almost all meet with sharp contempt. Wendy Shalit, whose *A Return to Modesty* is a cry for courtship and marriage rather than recreational sex, found herself belittled by the *Times*'s critic as "the self-appointed spokeswoman for the moral minority." Another *Times* reviewer tells us acidly that Stephanie Gutmann, whose *A Kinder, Gentler Military* gives chapter and verse on the crumbling of standards in the feminized military, "flies in the face of evidence—read Margaret Mead—that both women and men can be fierce in defending themselves."

Even more despised, if possible, are those who've made the case that Chira and her ilk find so deeply threatening: that children pay a devastating price when their mothers make them a lesser priority than their careers. When Danielle Crittenden passionately argued in *What Our Mothers Didn't Tell Us* that *Ms.*-era feminism had badly failed women by seeking to deny their innate desire for children and family, the *Times*'s critic dismissed her out of hand: "First, the good news: [this book] is very short." When the academic Elizabeth Fox Genovese's *Feminism Is Not the Story of My Life* conducted in-depth interviews with women around the country to make largely the same case and urge a more inclusive "family feminism," the *Times* called her exhaustively researched book "not really a sustained argument but a series of pronouncements reeled off at a manic pace." Many other works, such as ex-lawyer Carolyn Graglia's superb defense of traditional womanhood, *Domestic Tranquility: A Brief Against Feminism*, pass unmentioned in the *Times* at all and, as a result, tend to attract scant notice elsewhere.

Even on those rare occasions when a *Times* review takes a stance seemingly at odds with feminist orthodoxy, it can be counted on to rip conservative women who've held the same stance all along—thus, with characteristic audacity, letting those who'd had it wrong for so long off the hook. The publication this fall of psychologist Judith Wallerstein's *The Unexpected Legacy of Divorce* justly received lengthy and laudatory page-one treatment in the Sunday *Book Review*. Yet stuck in the piece, almost as a self-protective afterthought, was a single paragraph slamming Linda J. Waite and Maggie Gallagher's *The Case for Marriage*, which makes many of the same points. While Wallerstein (whose "goal," we are reassured, "is not to condemn divorce" and one of whose collaborators is "a regular contributor to *The New York Times*") is rightly celebrated for helping bring on the "dawning recognition" that divorce leaves deep and enduring scars on children, Waite and Gallagher, who never bought into the liberal fiction that happy divorced parents make happy kids, are somehow "less subtle and humane." Though they offer a wealth of evidence in support of marriage, "it's hard to know who is supposed to read this book or what purpose it might serve."

But feminists have never been able to shrug off Christina Hoff Sommers with such casual injustice. Because she was a well-regarded academic with a liberal pedigree, and because of the character of her attacks, she has from the start presented feminist stalwarts with a unique set of problems.

Drawn into the fight a decade or so ago, while a philosophy professor at Clark University in Worcester, Massachusetts, Sommers had been startled, then alarmed, by what she was hearing at feminist academic conferences—both the virulence of the anti-male, anti-family rhetoric and the shoddy thinking of those getting by as "feminist scholars." "These women would just toss around these ludicrous facts and figures," she recalls, "and no one ever challenged them—because if you did, you were branded a traitor and a reactionary, and your career was in jeopardy."

Her writings on academic feminism, more like insiders' reports, soon made her a pariah in that community; but it was the 1994 publication of her first book, *Who Stole Feminism?*, that turned the genial Sommers into feminism's Public Enemy No. 1. Chronicling the systematic radicalization of a noble concept—the legal and social equality of the sexes—by what she called "gender feminists," the book attacked the very foundations of the shaky feminist edifice, taking dead aim not only at the misbegotten feminist leadership but at an uncritical press that never called them to account. "To rally women to their cause," as she wrote of feminist zealotry, "it is not enough to remind us that many brutal and selfish men hurt women. They must persuade us that the system itself sanctions male brutality. They must convince us that the oppression of women, sustained from generation to generation, is a structural feature of our society."

What drew most attention to the book, and sent her foes into a defensive froth, was its focus on how feminist activists chronically abuse statistics in the propagation of their ideology. Particularly striking was the notice she called to the ludicrous claim—repeated in Gloria Steinem's *Revolution from Within* and Naomi Wolf's *The Beauty Myth* and dutifully broadcast by Ann Landers—that 150,000 American women die of anorexia every year. In fact, the number turned out to be fewer than 100. Then, too, there was the fantastic charge, made by NOW's Patricia Ireland and picked up by, among many others, the *Boston Globe*, the *Chicago Tribune*, and *Time* magazine, that domestic violence against pregnant women was responsible for more birth defects than all other causes combined. Dogged researcher though she is, in such cases Sommers didn't even have to break into a sweat to find the truth: on the phony birth defects story, all it took was a single phone call to the March of Dimes, ostensibly the source of the statistic, to elicit a firm "We have never seen this research before."

In a furious counteroffensive, feminist activists fell back on the tactics that had long proven so effective: they viciously attacked, distorting Sommers's record and views, seeking to portray her as far, far from the mainstream. "[Rush] Limbaugh, a proven font of disinformation, and Sommers—who portrays herself as a stickler for accuracy—have developed a mutual admiration society," sneered one of the several feminist newsletters that at the time devoted entire issues to Sommers. "Pat Buchanan declared that 'Ms. Sommers is right on the mark.'" The American Association of University Women, one of Sommers's principal targets, actually set up a "Christina Hotline," suggesting ways to discredit her. Gabrielle Lange, the AAUW's media relations director, later had the effrontery to compare her to a Holocaust denier.

It was against this backdrop that the *Times Book Review* weighed in. "On the evidence of this book," began its critique of *Who Stole Feminism?*, "Christina Hoff Sommers is a wallflower at feminist conferences. In revenge, she attends them obsessively." The book, it declared in conclusion, "is so overwrought and underargued that it is unlikely to amuse or persuade."

But to her foes' horror, this attack soon turned into just more evidence—indeed, the strongest yet—for Sommers's argument about the cozy relationship between the elite media and the over-the-top feminists it refused to monitor responsibly. The *Times* identified its reviewer, Nina Auerbach, as the John Welsh Centennial Professor of History and Literature at the University of Pennsylvania. What the *Book Review* neglected to mention is that she also happened to be herself one of those feminist conference speakers Sommers skewered in the book, not by name but clearly identifiable to anyone familiar with the event.

When this bit of deck-stacking came to light, it set off a storm of protest, and not only from conservatives. *Washington Post* media critic Howard Kurtz ran a column on the affair, entitled "At the N.Y. Times: A Review or Revenge?" In short order, the *Book Review* was moved to run a spate of letters from angry readers. "The *New York Times* should not assign books to partisan reviewers who are too ideologically or emotionally involved with the subject matter to give an objective opinion," noted one. "When I read Ms. Auerbach's hatchet job," said another, "I was appalled by the personal attacks against Ms. Sommers. Instead of reasoned disagreement, Ms. Auerbach delivered a vindictive tantrum."

Auerbach and Rebecca Sinkler, the editor of the *Times Book Review*, publicly responded that, in essence, the complaints about the review were little more than anti-feminist sour grapes, and Sommers's contention that the reviewer had to have recognized herself in the book was pure fantasy. "Auerbach is a good and lively writer," wrote Sinkler on AOL's *New York Times* service, "and she can be outspoken in her views. . . . We like that in a reviewer. . . . The *Book Review* received many letters asking us why we would assign the book to someone named in it. The answer is, we wouldn't."

But from a PR perspective, things didn't get any better for the *Times* when it got around that Nina Auerbach was not merely "a good and lively writer" but had once been Rebecca Sinkler's teacher at Penn. When Sinkler left the *Book Review* not long afterward, it was hard to find anyone who'd argue the episode wasn't a factor. If the *Times*'s bias on feminist matters had long been obvious to anyone who cared to see, rarely had it been quite so glaringly overt.

As these things go, the controversy only helped *Who Stole Feminism?*'s sales. In fact, for all the savagery of the attacks Sommers endured, the book has achieved what most of her adversaries, and most conservative writers, for that matter, can only dream of: it has "made a difference." Under increased scrutiny, in recent years feminist leaders have had to be far more careful about throwing around inflammatory and gaseous statistics.

Not, God knows, that they've lost any of their twisted ardor—we're not talking miracles. Indeed, a compelling case can be made that for all the damage they've done to the culture over the past several decades, their most recent fixation— on boys—has been the most insidious yet.

For in the feminist worldview, notwithstanding their remarkable success in mainstreaming their ideology in offices and the military, at colleges and in TV sitcoms, things are not yet nearly as they should be. Males are still too traditionally . . . male. They're still too aggressive; they still like to play rough and lack sensitivity and "objectify" females. The solution? Since, according to doctrine, all such behavior is learned, a product of our sick culture, it must be attacked at its very root.

In brief, boys too are victims of patriarchy. We must systematically reprogram them—to be more like girls.

This is the doctrine that Sommers exposes and eviscerates in *The War Against Boys*—which, given its potential to engage otherwise apolitical mothers and fathers, arguably makes the new book even more dangerous to the zealots than was her first. Herself the mother of sons, Sommers appeals both to the head and the gut. "It is," as she writes, "a story of how we are turning against boys and forgetting a simple truth: that the energy, competitiveness, and corporal daring of normal, decent males are responsible for much of what is right in the world."

Obviously, ordinary people never stopped knowing that; as Chico Marx might've said of the feminists' relentless effort to have parents force dolls on indifferent little boys, "You gonna believe me or your own eyes?" And yet the book makes clear just how deeply, in the name of "gender equity," the anti-boy campaign has taken hold and how horrifying are its consequences in the real world.

Launched in earnest in the early nineties, the "gender equity" crusade came about largely in reaction to the work of one woman, feminist superstar Carol Gilligan of Harvard's Graduate School of Education. It was Gilligan who, as Sommers observes, via "groundbreaking studies" and best-selling books, "initiated the thinking about American girls as victimized, silenced Ophelias" and gave "intellectual respectability to reformers' efforts to reconstruct children's gender identities."

The essence of the Gilligan message on what the culture allegedly does to girls is summed up by the title of a characteristically laudatory *New York Times Magazine* profile that appeared in 1990: "Confident at 11, Confused at 16." Why, in early adolescence, do girls typically (in Gilligan's classic formulation) "lose their voice" and "go underground"? Basically, because they learn that to get by in a patriarchal world, it is best to be passive and submissive. Because, in fact, even within the confines of their own narrow world, they routinely find themselves shouted down in class by overly aggressive boys and ignored by boy-friendly teachers. A much-quoted re-

port by the American Association of University Women entitled "How Schools Shortchange Girls" soon lent even greater
authority to this idea, as did feminist academics like Myra and
David Sadker, who wrote ominously of the schools' "secret
sexist lessons and the quiet losses they engender."

As we know, in short order, network magazine shows and
alarmist newspaper headlines were proclaiming the "crisis."
True to form, the *Times* helped lead the way, proving particularly cooperative in promoting the holiday created by the
Ms. Foundation to combat the collapse of female adolescent
self-esteem. To date, Take Our Daughters to Work Day has
garnered—count 'em—sixty-one breathless mentions in the
paper's pages.

But for those pushing the gender equity line, the key goal
was legislative action, and that drive proved successful even
beyond their most fevered dreams. By early 1994 Congress had
passed, and Bill Clinton had signed, the Equity in Education
Act, mandating gender-neutral textbooks and an end to sexual
harassment at all school levels, and providing federal funds
for the creation of an office of women's equity in the Department of Education to ensure that the feminist slant on things
got a full hearing in texts and curricula.

Through it all, for all the attention they got, critics of the
movement appeared not to exist. Only now did scattered reports appear, questioning if all this was really fair to boys.
Most of these reports questioned whether the Take Our
Daughters holiday ought to be expanded to include all children, an idea fiercely opposed by the Ms. Foundation. After
all, by most key indicators—dropout rates and numbers of re-
medial students, suicide rates and percentages going on to
college—wasn't it young males who were really in greatest
jeopardy? Such a turn finally forced the feminists to address
the boy issue directly: and this they have done with chilling

resolve. Yes, they observed, boys are not healthy for girls and other living things, but ultimately it is not their fault, for society pressures them to conform to a soul-deadening, emotion-suppressing, female-subordinating definition of masculinity. And this, too, is a "crisis," calling for emergency measures.

In coming up with a solution, the feminists (as Lionel Trilling might have put it) seem to have taken as their manual Ferdinand the Bull, the children's tale that drives home its anti-macho message with sledgehammer delicacy. Just as Ferdinand accepts that he is a superior being for choosing to smell flowers instead of fight, so, in essence, the feminists declare boys' deranged "bull" nature to be merely a social construct, ugly but changeable.

Thus have they confidently moved to remake the educational system—indeed, the entire culture—to that end. From the earliest age, boys are to be subjected to a program aimed at stripping them of aggression, boisterousness, and irreverence.

In her book, Sommers relates in harrowing detail the extent to which this program is already in place. The key feminist hysteric she describes is someone almost no one has heard of: Katherine Hanson, who runs the Women's Educational Equity Act Publishing Center, and whose beliefs about the malevolence of the patriarchy are truly stunning. Among other things, Hanson has publicly charged that nearly four million women are beaten to death by men annually, which, if you're counting, makes eleven thousand a day, forty million a decade—basically, before long, every female in America. (The actual total of women murdered in the United States in 1996 was 3,631—most by complete strangers, some even by other women.)

It is to Hanson whom the Department of Education, under the Equity in Education Act, has given responsibility for providing "gender-fair" study materials to the nation's schools.

Believing as she does that "our educational system is a primary carrier of the dominant culture's assumptions," she has inundated teachers and schoolchildren with literature portraying normal boys as would-be batterers, harassers, and rapists. Her anti-harassment teacher manuals bear such titles as *Quit It!*, aimed at grades K-3 and, for slightly older children, *Girls and Boys Getting Along: Teaching Sexual Harassment Prevention in the Elementary Classroom*.

A friend of mine who's getting a teaching credential in Connecticut tells of finding himself, the very first week of that state's accreditation program, having to endure a lecture from one of the legions of "gender equity specialists" who now pervade the educational scene. "She went on for nearly an hour about anti-girl bias by teachers, how they start off so well, then fall behind in high school when teachers show favoritism to boys. So at the end I raised my hand and, politely as I could, asked why girls did so much better than boys in the earlier grades: could it be that elementary school teachers, who are overwhelmingly female, are biased in their favor? Or might there simply be differences in the ways boys and girls develop? She got furious, started going on how we men always got defensive, basically refusing to answer what she took to be a sexist question." My friend shook his head. "Afterward, four or five people very quietly thanked me—they agreed it was flat-out propaganda, incredibly unfair to boys. But of course, not one of them had spoken up. That's what they've done, spread this fear by defining honest conversation about this as evidence of bigotry."

But what's even more jarring is seeing how the spreading anti-boy ethic gets played out in the lives of ordinary people. Indeed, after years of alarmist reports, the presumption that schools chronically shortchange girls has taken hold for millions of well-meaning souls who have never heard of Carol

Gilligan. Just recently, I met a woman, a nurse at a local hospital, who waxed passionate on the subject. With a daughter about to turn thirteen, she was desperate to get her into an all-girl private school and thus rescue her from the dire consequences of being a female in a mixed-sex environment. "This is when they start to lose their self-esteem," she explained soberly. "There are all these studies."

Almost as much as the feminist furies themselves, the *Times* and other voices of elite culture are responsible for the spread of this pernicious nonsense—now promoting the phony self-esteem crisis, now pathologizing boyhood. Indeed, for book reviewers at the paper of record, sympathy for boys is now okay—more than okay—as long as the target is nurture and not nature.

The maestro of this genre has been Gilligan acolyte William Pollack, author of the best-seller *Real Boys*. Pollack got particular attention in the wake of the Columbine tragedy, appearing incessantly on the tube (he was a regular on "Oprah"), arguing that the lunatic killers were not, in fact, grotesque aberrations but products of the same system that afflicts millions of young men who pass as normal. "If we don't allow boys to cry tears," as he put it to one sympathetic reporter at the time, "they're going to cry bullets."

Unsurprisingly, when Sommers's book appeared this past spring, defending traditional boyhood and deriding the weeny masculinity the feminists hold up as an ideal, the press largely cold-shouldered it. It went unreviewed in the *Los Angeles Times*, the *Chicago Tribune*, the *Boston Globe*, and many other papers.

But, true to form, the *Times* took on *The War Against Boys* the last Sunday in June.

The big news was not the review's content—dismissive, it all but ignored the book's central argument—but the identity of its author, child psychiatrist Robert Coles. For, incredibly enough, history seemed to be repeating itself, since Coles is a Harvard Ed School colleague of Sommers's adversary Gilligan, among the book's primary targets.

Moreover, Coles's piece simultaneously reviewed, far more favorably, the new book co-authored by Sommers's other foe Pollack—who's also affiliated with Harvard. Sommers "speaks of our children," observed Coles testily, "yet she hasn't sought them out; instead she attends [to] those who have, in fact, worked with boys and girls—and in so doing is quick to look askance at Carol Gilligan's ideas about girls and William Pollack's about boys. Much of *The War Against Boys* comes across as Sommers's strongly felt war against these two prominent psychologists, who have spent years trying to learn how young men and women grow to adulthood in the United States."

Again, it was left to readers of the *Book Review* to call its editors to account. "Dare we hope that a book like Christina Hoff Sommers's *War Against Boys* might be given full and fair treatment?" demanded historian Stanley Kurtz in a published letter. "Apparently not. Not only is the review of Sommers bundled with a review of William S. Pollack, one of her adversaries, but the reviewer himself, Robert Coles, is a Harvard colleague of both Pollack and Sommers's other chief antagonist, Carol Gilligan."

This is how matters stood when, a few weeks later, Richard Bernstein's review of *The War Against Boys* turned up in the daily *Times*. Appearing to have read an entirely different book from what Coles read, Bernstein wrote that Sommers makes her arguments "persuasively and unflinchingly, and with plenty of data to support them," and adding, in a keenly heartfelt conclusion, that her work is less polemic than entreaty. "There is a crying in the wilderness quality to her book, a sense that certain simple truths have been lost sight of in the smoky quarrelsomeness of American life."

One need hardly be a conspiracy theorist to conjure up a link between Bernstein's piece and Coles's embarrassing earlier one—or, for that matter, with the even more shockingly unfair one of several years earlier. Even the most arrogant pooh-bahs at the *Times* must be at least dimly aware by now that, in its boundless enthusiasm for the multiculturalist agenda, the paper has squandered much of its treasured credibility. "When people around here see something on feminism in the *Times*," as my friend Dennis Boyles, who once worked as an editor at the Sunday *Times Magazine*, puts it, "their first impulse is to say, 'Wait, is this really true?'"

But just as likely, the review was a lonely act of personal valor. Bernstein has for some time been a rare beacon of standards and common sense at the paper—someone, indeed, who himself has written at book length about the ills of multiculturalism (and in the process learned how it feels to be reviewed unfairly in his own paper).

In the ongoing fight against the culture's entrenched ideologues, progress comes about incrementally: as individuals, often at real personal cost, continue to tell the truth, it begins to be heard. The tenor of the national conversation might begin to alter subtly merely because the *Times* has alerted its broad and overwhelmingly liberal readership to the possibility that what they've been told for years on the subject is false. In fact, most adolescent girls are not hurting and vulnerable; rather, it is their male counterparts who are truly under siege. This insight might give at least momentary pause in a government office or corporate boardroom the next time a project aimed at fiddling with the lives of young men and women rears its malformed head, and even more to the point, it might change the thinking in innumerable private homes.

I got just a hint of this myself a few days after the piece appeared, when I ran again into the nurse with the thirteen-year-old daughter. Having read the review, she was confused—already a step in the right direction—and planning to buy Sommers's book. "You really just don't know who to believe anymore," she said. "I'm just going to have to look into this for myself."

[2000]

MODERN MANHOOD

Feminists have harped and harpied on about the position of women in modern societies. But what about the men? The radical changes in sexual mores, patterns of employment, and domestic life have turned their lives upside down. Men now encounter women not as "the weaker sex" but as equal competitors in the public sphere—the sphere where men used to be in charge. And in the private sphere, where an ancient division of labor once gave guidance to those who crossed its threshold, there is no knowing what strategy will be most effective. Manly gestures—holding open a door for a woman, handing her into an automobile, taking charge of her bags—can spark insulted rejection; displays of wealth, power, or influence are likely to seem ridiculous to a woman who herself has more of them; and the disappearance of female modesty and sexual restraint has made it hard for a man to believe, when a woman yields to his advances, that her doing so is a special tribute to his masculine powers, rather than a day-to-day transaction, in which he, like the last one, is dispensable.

The sexual revolution is not the only cause of men's confusion. Social, political, and legal changes have shrunk the all-male sphere to the vanishing point, redefining every activity in which men once proved that they were indispensable, so that now women can do the job, too—or at any rate appear to do it. Feminists have sniffed out male pride wherever it has grown and ruthlessly uprooted it. Under their pressure, modern culture has downgraded or rejected such masculine virtues as courage, tenacity, and military prowess in favor of more gentle, more "socially inclusive" habits. The advent of in vitro fertilization and the promise of cloning create the impression that men are not even necessary for human reproduction, while the growth of the single-parent household—in which the mother is the only adult, and the state is too often the only provider—has made fatherless childhood into an increasingly common option. These changes threaten to make manhood redundant, and many children now grow up to acknowledge no source of love, authority, or guidance apart from the mother, whose men come and go like seasonal laborers, drifting through the matriarchal realm with no prospect of a permanent position.

The unhappiness of men flows directly from the collapse of their old social role as protectors and providers. For the feminists, this old social role was a way of confining women to the household, where they would not compete for the benefits available outside. Its destruction, they contend, is therefore a liberation—not of women only, but of men, too, who can now choose whether they wish to assert themselves in the public sphere or whether, on the contrary, they wish to stay at home with the baby (which may very well be someone else's baby). This is the core idea of feminism—that "gender roles" are not natural but cultural, and that by changing them we can overthrow old power structures and achieve new and more creative ways of being.

The feminist view is orthodoxy throughout the American academy, and it is the premise of all legal and political thinking among the liberal elite, which dissidents oppose at peril of their reputations or careers. Nevertheless, a groundswell of resistance to it is gathering force among anthropologists and sociobiologists. Typical is Lionel Tiger, who three decades ago coined the term "male bonding" to denote something that all men need and that few now get. It wasn't social convention that dictated the traditional roles of man and woman, Tiger suggests; instead, the millions of years of evolution that formed our species made us what we are. You can make men pretend to be less dominant and less aggressive; you can make them pretend to accept a subordinate role in domestic life and a dependent position in society. But deep down, in the instinctual flow of life that is manhood itself, they will rebel. The unhappiness of men, Tiger argues, comes from this deep and unconfessed conflict between social pretense and sexual necessity. And when manhood finally breaks out—as it inevitably will—it is in distorted and dangerous forms, like the criminal gangs of the modern city or the swaggering misogyny of the city slicker.

Tiger sees sex as a biological phenomenon, whose deep explanation lies in the theory of sexual selection. Each of us, he believes, acts in obedience to a strategy built into our genes, which seek their own perpetuity through our sexual behavior. The genes of a woman, who is vulnerable in childbirth and needs support during years of child-rearing thereafter, call for a mate who will protect her and her offspring. The genes of a man require a guarantee that the children he provides for are his own, lest all his labor be (from the genes' point of view) wasted. Hence nature itself, working through our genes, decrees a division of roles between the sexes. It predisposes men to fight for territory, to protect their women, to drive away rivals, and to strive for status and recognition in the public world—the world where men conflict. It predisposes women to be faithful, private, and devoted to the home. Both these dispositions involve the working out of long-term genetic strategies—strategies that it is not for us to change, since we are the effect and not the cause of them.

The feminists, of course, will have none of this. Biology may indeed assign us a sex, in the form of this or that organ. But much more important than our sex, they say, is our "gender"—and gender is a cultural construct, not a biological fact.

The term "gender" comes from grammar, where it is used to distinguish masculine from feminine nouns. By importing it into the discussion of sex, feminists imply that our sex roles are as man-made and therefore malleable as syntax. Gender includes the rituals, habits, and images through which we represent ourselves to one another as sexual beings. It is not sex but the consciousness of sex. Hitherto, say the feminists, the "gender identity" of women is something that men have imposed upon them. The time has come for women to forge their own gender identity, to remake their sexuality as a sphere of freedom rather than a sphere of bondage.

Taken to extremes—and feminism takes everything to extremes—the theory reduces sex to a mere appearance, with gender as the reality. If, having forged your true gender identity, you find yourself housed in the wrong kind of body, then it is the body that must change. If you believe yourself to be a woman, then you are a woman, notwithstanding the fact that you have the body of a man. Hence medical practitioners, instead of regarding sex-change operations as a gross violation of the body and indeed a kind of criminal assault, now endorse them, and in England the National Health Service pays for them. Gender, in the feminists' radical conception of it, begins to sound like a dangerous fantasy, rather like the genetic theories of Lysenko, Stalin's favorite biologist, who argued that acquired characteristics could be inherited, so that man could mold his own nature with almost infinite plasticity. Perhaps we should replace the old question that James Thurber put before us at the start of the sexual revolution with a new equivalent: not "Is Sex Necessary?" but "Is Gender Possible?"

In a certain measure, however, the feminists are right to distinguish sex from gender and to imply that we are free to revise our images of the masculine and the feminine. After all, the sociobiologists' argument accurately describes the similarities between people and apes, but it ignores the differences. Animals in the wild are slaves of their genes. Human beings in society are not. The whole point of culture is that it makes us something more than creatures of mere biology and sets us on the road to self-realization. Where in sociobiology is the self, its choices and its fulfillment? Surely the sociobiologists are wrong to think that our genes alone determined the traditional sex roles.

But just as surely are the feminists wrong to believe that we are completely liberated from our biological natures and that the traditional sex roles emerged only from a social power struggle in which men were victorious and women enslaved. The traditional roles existed in order to humanize our genes and also to control them. The masculine and feminine were ideals, through which the animal was transfigured into the personal. Sexual morality was an attempt to transform a genetic need into a personal relation. It existed precisely to stop men from scattering their seed through the tribe, and to prevent women from accepting wealth and power, rather than love, as the signal for reproduction. It was the cooperative answer to a deep-seated desire, in both man and woman, for the "helpmeet" who will make life meaningful.

In other words, men and women are not merely biological organisms. They are also moral beings. Biology sets limits to our behavior but does not dictate it. The arena formed by our instincts merely defines the possibilities among which we must choose if we are to gain the respect, acceptance, and love of one another. Men and women have shaped themselves not merely for the purpose of reproduction but in order to bring dignity and kindness to the relations between them. To this end, they have been in the business of creating and re-creating the masculine and the feminine ever since they realized that the relations between the sexes must be established by negotiation and consent, rather than by force. The difference between traditional morality and modern feminism is that the first wishes to enhance and to humanize the difference between the sexes, while the second wishes to discount or even annihilate it. In that sense, feminism really is against nature.

Yet at the same time, feminism seems an inevitable response to the breakdown of the traditional sexual morality. People readily accepted the traditional roles when honor and decency sustained them. But why should women trust men, now that men are so quick to discard their obligations? Marriage was once permanent and safe; it offered the woman social status and protection, long after she ceased to be sexually attractive. And it provided a sphere in which she was dominant. The sacrifice permanent marriage demanded of men made tolerable to women the male monopoly over the public realm, in which men competed for money and social rewards. The two sexes respected each other's territory and recognized that each must renounce something for their mutual benefit. Now that men in the wake of the sexual revolution feel free to be serially polygamous, women have no secure territory of their own. They have no choice, therefore, but to capture what they can of the territory once monopolized by men.

It was one of the great discoveries of civilization that men do not gain acceptance from women by brashly displaying their manhood in aggressive and violating gestures. But they do gain acceptance by being gentlemen. The gentleman was not a person with feminine gender and masculine sex. He was through and through a man. But he was also gentle—in all the senses of that lucent word. He was not belligerent but courageous, not possessive but protective, not aggressive to other men but bold, even-tempered, and ready to agree on terms. He was animated by a sense of honor—which meant taking responsibility for his actions and shielding those who depended on him. And his most important attribute was loyalty, which implied that he would not deny his obligations merely because he was in a position to profit from doing so. Much of the anger of women toward men has come about because the ideal of the gentleman is now so close to extinction. Popular entertainment has only one image of manhood to put before the young: and it is an image of untrammeled aggression, in which automatic weapons play a major part, and in which gentleness in whatever form appears as a weakness rather than as a strength. How far this is from those epics of courtly love, which set in motion the European attempt to rescue manhood from biology and reshape it as a moral idea, needs no elaboration.

It was not only the upper classes that idealized the relation between the sexes or moralized their social roles. In the working-class community from which my father's family came, the old mutuality was part of the routine of domestic life, encapsulated in recognized displays of masculine and feminine virtue. One such was the Friday-night ritual of the wage packet. My grandfather would come home and place on the kitchen table the unopened envelope containing his wages. My grandmother would pick it up and empty it into her wallet, handing back two shillings for drink. Grandfather would then go to the pub and drink himself into a state of proud self-assertion among his peers. If women came to the pub they would linger in the doorway, communicating by messenger with the smoke-filled rooms inside but respecting the threshold of this masculine arena as though it were guarded by angels.

My grandfather's gesture, as he laid down his wage packet on the kitchen table, was imbued with a peculiar grace: it was a recognition of my grandmother's importance as a woman, of her right to his consideration and of her value as the mother of his children. Likewise, her waiting outside the pub until closing time, when he would be too unconscious to suffer the humiliation of it, before transporting him home in a wheelbar-row, was a gesture replete with feminine considerateness. It was her way of recognizing his inviolable sovereignty as a wage earner and a man.

Courtesy, courtliness, and courtship were so many doors into the court of love, where human beings moved as in a pag-eant. My grandparents were excluded by their proletarian way of life from all other forms of courtliness, which is why this one was so important. It was their opening to an enchant-ment that they could obtain in no other way. My grandfather had little to recommend him to my grandmother other than his strength, good looks, and manly deportment. But he re-spected the woman in her and played the role of gentleman as best he could whenever he escorted her outside the home. Hence my grandmother, who disliked him intensely—for he was ignorant, complacent, and drunk, and stood across the threshold of her life as an immovable obstacle to social ad-vancement—nevertheless loved him passionately as a man. This love could not have lasted were it not for the mystery of gender. My grandfather's masculinity set him apart in a sov-ereign sphere of his own, just as my grandmother's femininity protected her from his aggression. All that they knew of virtue they had applied to the task of remaining to some measure mysterious to each other. And in this they succeeded, as they succeeded in little else.

A similar division of spheres occurred throughout society, and in every corner of the globe. But marriage was its pivotal institution, and marriage depended upon fidelity and sexual restraint. Marriages lasted not only because divorce was disapproved of but also because marriage was preceded by an extended period of courtship, in which love and trust could take root before sexual experiment. This period of courtship was also one of display, in which men showed off their manliness and women their femininity. And this is what we mean, or ought to mean, by the "social construction" of gender. By playacting, the two partners readied themselves for their future roles, learning to admire and cherish the separateness of their natures. The courting man gave glamour to the masculine character, just as the courting woman gave mystery to the feminine. And something of this glamour and mystery remained thereafter, a faint halo of enchantment that caused each to encourage the other in the apartness that they both admired.

The Taming of the Shrew and *Romeo and Juliet,* Jane Austen and George Eliot, Henry James and Charlotte Brontë, all have matchlessly described all that, as has D. H. Lawrence (in its lower-class version) in his stories. This literature shows what is missing from sociobiology. Marriage does not merely serve the reproductive strategies of our genes; it serves the reproductive need of society. It also serves the individual in his pursuit of a life and fulfillment of his own. Its capacity for ordering and sanctifying erotic love goes beyond anything required by our genes. As our Enlightenment morality rightly insists, we are also free beings, whose experience is through and through qualified by our sense of moral value. We do not respond to one another as animals but as persons—which means that, even in sexual desire, freedom of choice is essential to the aim. The object of desire must be treated, in Kant's famous words, not as a means only but as an end. Hence true sexual desire is desire for a person, and not for sex, conceived as a generalized commodity. We surround the sexual act with constraints and interdictions that are in no way dictated by the species, precisely so as to focus our thoughts and desires on the free being rather than the bodily mechanism. In this we are immeasurably superior to our genes, whose attitude to what is happening is, by comparison, mere pornography.

Even when the sacramental view of marriage began to wane, mankind still held erotic feelings apart, as things too intimate for public discussion, which could only be soiled by their display. Chastity, modesty, shame, and passion were part of an artificial but necessary drama. The erotic was idealized in order that marriage should endure. And marriage, construed as our parents and grandparents construed it, was both a source of personal fulfillment and the principal way in which one generation passed on its social and moral capital to the next.

It was that vision of marriage, as a lifelong existential commitment, that lay behind the process of "gender construction" in the days when men were tamed and women idealized. If marriage is no longer safe, however, girls are bound to look elsewhere for their fulfillment. And elsewhere means the public sphere—for it is a sphere dominated by strangers, with clear rules and procedures, in which you can defend yourself from exploitation. The advantage of inhabiting this sphere needs no explaining to a girl whose abandoned mother lies grieving upstairs. Nor do her experiences at school or college teach her to trust or respect the male character. Her sex education classes have taught her that men are to be used and discarded like the condoms that package them. And the feminist ideology has encouraged her to think that only one thing matters—which is to discover and fulfill her true gender identity while discarding the false gender identity that the "patriarchal culture" has foisted upon her. Just as boys become men without becoming manly, therefore, so do girls become women without becoming feminine. Modesty and chastity are dismissed as politically incorrect; and in every sphere where they encounter men, women meet them as competitors. The voice that calmed the violence of manhood—namely, the female call for protection—has been consigned to silence.

Just as the feminine virtues existed in order to make men gentle, however, so manliness existed in order to break down the reserve that caused women to withhold their favors until security was in sight. In the world of "safe sex," those old habits seem tedious and redundant. In consequence, there has arisen another remarkable phenomenon in America: the litigiousness of women toward the men they have slept with. It seems as though consent, offered so freely and without regard for the preliminaries once assumed to be indispensable, is not really consent and can be withdrawn retroactively. The charges of harassment or even "date rape" lie always in reserve. The slap in the face that used to curtail importunate advances is now offered after the event, and in a far more deadly form—a form no longer private, intimate, and remediable but public, regimented, and with the absolute objectivity of law. You might take this as showing that "safe sex" is really sex at its most dangerous. Maybe marriage is the only safe sex that we know.

When Stalin imposed Lysenko's theories upon the Soviet Union, as the "scientific" basis of his effort to remold human nature and form it into the "New Soviet Man," the human economy continued, hidden away beneath the mad imperatives of the Stalinist state. And a black sexual economy persists in modern America, which no feminist policing has yet succeeded in stamping out. Men go on taking charge of things, and women go on deferring to the men. Girls still want to be mothers and to obtain a father for their children; boys still want to impress the other sex with their prowess and their power. The steps from attraction to consummation may be short, but they are steps in which the old roles and the old desires hover at the edge of things.

Hence nothing is more interesting to the visiting anthropologist than the antics of American college students: the girl who, in the midst of some foulmouthed feminist diatribe, suddenly begins to blush; or the boy who, walking with his girlfriend, puts out an arm to protect her. The sociobiologists tell us that these gestures are dictated by the species. We should see them, rather, as revelations of the moral sense. They are the sign that there really is a difference between the masculine and the feminine, over and above the difference between the male and the female. Without the masculine and the feminine, indeed, sex loses its meaning. Gender is not just possible but necessary.

And here, surely, lies our hope for the future. When women forge their own "gender identity," in the way the feminists recommend, they become unattractive to men—or attractive only as sex objects, not as individual persons. And when men cease to be gentlemen, they become unattractive to women. Sexual companionship then goes from the world. All that it needs to save young people from this predicament is for old-fashioned moralists to steal unobserved past their feminist guardians and whisper the truth into eager and astonished ears—the truth that gender is indeed a construct, but one that involves both sexes, acting in mutual support, if it is to be built successfully. In my experience, young people hear with great sighs of relief that the sexual revolution may have been a mistake, that women are allowed to be modest, and that men can make a shot at being gentlemen.

And this is what we should expect. If we are free beings, it is because, unlike our genes, we can hear the truth and decide what to do about it.

[1999]

RESOLUTION

ROGER SCRUTON

BRING BACK STIGMA

It is now orthodox to regard social stigma as a form of oppression, to be discarded on our collective quest for inner freedom. But the political philosophers and novelists of former times would have been horrified by such a view. In almost all matters that touched upon the core requirements of social order, they believed that the genial pressure of manners, morals, and customs—enforced by the various forms of disapproval, stigma, shame, and reproach—was a more powerful guarantor of civilized and lawful behavior than the laws themselves. Inner sanctions, they argued, more dependably maintain society than such external ones as policemen and courts. That is why the moralists of the eighteenth century, for example, rarely touched upon murder, theft, rape, or criminal deception; instead they were passionately interested in the small-scale mores on which social order depends and which, properly adhered to, make such crimes unthinkable.

Stigma has evaporated in our era, and along with it much of the constant, small-scale self-regulation of the community, which depends on each individual's respect for, and fear of, other people's judgment. In consequence, the laws have expanded, both in extent and complexity, to fill the void. Yet as sanctions have been expropriated from society by the state, people feel far more free to follow their own inclinations, to disregard proprieties, and to ignore the effect of their behavior on others and on the common good. For although the law impinges far more on their lives, they experience it as an external force with no real moral authority. In addition, the law increasingly distinguishes the "public" realm, where it is the sole objective authority, from the "private" realm, where it cannot intrude, leaving the private realm less and less regulated, despite the fact that it contains most of the matters on which the future of society depends: sexual conduct, the rearing of children, honest dealing, and self-respect.

Moreover, there is no evidence that the law can really compensate for the loss of social sanctions. The law combats crime not by eliminating criminal schemes but by increasing the risk attached to them; stigma combats crime by creating people who have no criminal schemes in the first place. The steady replacement of stigma by law, therefore, is a key cause of the constant increase in the number and severity of crimes.

Half a century ago, anthropologist Ruth Benedict famously distinguished societies according to whether their citizens' inner lives were governed by shame or by guilt, the first directed outward to society, the second directed inward to the self. But this is a distinction without a difference, guilt being simply the inner residue of shame. Guilt is a learned response—an internalization of the disapproval, anger, and ostracism that parents, teachers, and neighbors direct toward the unruly child to mold his conscience. Guilt exists therefore only where people fear adverse judgment. The evidence from modern societies suggests that, where the community ceases to respond to moral faults with public sanctions, individuals cease to feel guilty about them, and conscience weakens. If we wish for inner sanctions to exist, we must back them up with sanctions of a more public and outward-going kind. Moral norms, generated collectively, must also be collectively imposed.

Sexual morality provides a particularly clear and important case in point. Sex is the bond of society and also the force that explodes it. Properly managed, sexual feelings lead to lasting marriages, stable families, children with vigilant parents, and the handing down from generation to generation of the precious store of social capital. Mismanaged, they lead to a society—perhaps one should say "society"—of casual encounters, jealousies, and aggressions, in which there are neither lasting commitments nor sacrifices on behalf of children.

Society makes sexual behavior a matter of conscience, thus regulating it more effectively. And this moralization of sexual feeling also transforms it, creating feelings that are not only uniquely human but vital to our happiness. Erotic love, in contrast with animal lust, requires distance and the overcoming of distance by passion. This distance does not exist in a society where sexual release is obtainable anywhere and from anyone without the penalty of guilt or shame, enforced through stigma and ostracism. By imbuing sexual feelings with psychological sanctions, traditional societies ensured that they were controlled by the person who feels them. As a result, sexual feelings were integrated into moral character, not governed from outside by laws and regulations but from inside by the will. This inward control set people at a distance from one another; it also made them safe to one another by ensuring that sexual advances were not just smash-and-grab raids aimed at the goods in the window but the first steps toward love and commitment. Take this inner control away, and what was previously a source of social cohesion becomes the cause of social decay.

Long ago, societies recognized that they could not make adultery or out-of-wedlock childbearing into crimes without opening the way to intolerable injustices; Christ himself took the first step toward decriminalization when he ironically invited anyone who was without sin to begin stoning the woman accused of adultery. Nevertheless, even as the law withdrew from these areas, the moral code remained, and communities were able to protect themselves from the sexual excesses that threatened their existence by stigmatizing those who indulged in them. Take away the stigma and we are left with no socially accepted means for enforcing sexual morality.

This loss is especially significant now, as we begin to wake up to the damage that the collapse of marriage has inflicted on society. The stable, two-parent family no longer seems an eccentricity or a peculiarity of "bourgeois" society. Increasingly we acknowledge it as the institution that secured the stability, harmony, and prosperity of Western societies and that enabled one generation to bequeath its culture and institutions to the next. Marriage was kept in place not by law but by stigma, which ensured that most babies, even if not conceived in wedlock, were at least born in it, thus enjoying the social acceptance and the parental nurture that children need if they are to grow up to be secure and decent citizens.

Of course, the stigmatization of illegitimacy had cruel side effects—not least upon the children ridiculed as "bastards." My grandfather was one of them, and the stigma ensured that, like Richard III, he came into the world "determined to prove a villain"—a determination he amply fulfilled. But as James Q. Wilson and others have shown, the removal of illegitimacy's stigma, however kindly intended, has done nothing to improve the character and prospects of illegitimate children. Statistical studies of American prisoners, for example, show that illegitimacy is by far the most important factor in disposing children to a life of crime—more significant than IQ, race, culture, or any other factor investigated by the criminologists. The function of the stigma was to prevent people from reproducing in socially destructive ways. With stigma gone, more and more children are now born out of wedlock; and welfare support to single mothers makes it economically advantageous for young women to take this shortcut to reproductive success. This is a catastrophe in today's inner cities; in Britain it will be a still bigger catastrophe in twenty years' time, when children born in wedlock will be in the minority.

The case is not very different with adultery. People of my parents' generation would not publicly confess to this transgression; if they committed it, they did so in secret. Known adulterers were the subject of malicious gossip, and never would they flaunt their passion in public. Politicians could still be shamed, and their careers ruined, if their adulterous liaisons came to light. Today, however, someone invited to a dinner party with his wife might turn up instead with his mistress—even a mistress whom nobody yet knows—without precipitating anything more than mild curiosity.

The effect on marriage is evident. In Britain, as in America, nearly half of all marriages now embarked on will end in divorce, and in the kind of polite society inhabited by our urban elite, marriage has no more legitimacy and invites no greater public respect than a casual liaison. Official documents have been revised to put "partner" in the place of "spouse," removing marriage from its privileged position in the official culture. Marriage is no longer the socially accepted norm marking the true conclusion of sexual development, but an individual choice, the business of no one save the couple who embark on it.

Hence no shame now attaches to divorce. Serial polygamy is the norm among successful men, and those who lose out from this state of affairs—the women and children whom they abandon—have been deprived of their most important protection, which was the social penalties suffered by the malefactor. Our society lavishes much sentimental sympathy on imaginary victims, whose feckless behavior is the real cause of their misfortune, but it is utterly indifferent to the real victims, such as illegitimate or abandoned children, whose misfortune results from its own refusal to cast judgment on the wrongdoers.

Transgressions were not neatly divided into offenses in law, to be dealt with only by the law, and offenses to propriety, to be dealt with by social rebuke. Some forms of behavior—dishonesty, for example—came into both categories and could be effectively controlled only by a combination of punishment and social rejection. And the convicted criminal was invariably shamed for his behavior and either ostracized or required to live in a state of penance. This made sense, since the real purpose of shaming is not to punish crimes but to create the kind of people who don't commit them. The criminal therefore had to be held up as an example from which the rest of society could learn.

But stigma is now retreating even from crime. Convicted thieves and burglars are no longer automatically excluded from social gatherings. Indeed, some (such as the English criminal Howard Marks) have acquired kudos from writing about their "hotheaded youth" and the jolly times they had as drug dealers, robbers, or burglars. And if the crime can be represented as an assault on the institutions of bourgeois society, rehabilitation is all the more easy to obtain. A case in point is Nick Leeson, an employee of Baring's Bank (itself a symbol of the old dignity and probity of the City of London) who deceptively squandered the funds entrusted to him and as a result destroyed this venerable institution and the many lives that depended on it. After serving time in a Singapore jail, Leeson returned to England to become a media star, giving interviews and writing articles, enjoying his moment of celebrity and being handsomely paid for it. Even violent criminals, provided they have "done their time" and so have "paid their debt to society," can enjoy a hero's welcome when they travel to foreign parts, as did rapist Mike Tyson on his recent visit to Britain.

In Britain the leading charity devoted to the treatment of criminals is called the National Society for the Care and Rehabilitation of Offenders. Its purpose is to make punishment the prerogative of the state and to neutralize the desire of society to provide supplementary punishments of its own. Not "criminals" but "offenders"; not "punishment" but "care" and "rehabilitation"—or, to use the British politically correct expression, "social inclusion." No stigma should attach to the criminal on account of his crime: the law punishes him according to its neutral and objective calculus. Our only role thereafter is to forgive and forget, to "rehabilitate," on the assumption that the debt has been paid. And by thinking of crime in this way, you vastly increase its likelihood, since you remove the real motive for good behavior, which is the fear of judgment. When the response to the criminal is not rebuke but rehabilitation, crime is de-moralized, voided of blame, to become a market in which deeds are judged by their price, not their value. The price of rape is seven years; and when the price is paid, you are back, like Mike Tyson, on display.

We think of the assault on stigma as beginning with the great dramas of Protestant guilt—with Hawthorne's *Scarlet Letter*, say, or Ibsen's *John Gabriel Borkman*—but it is already there in the Enlightenment emphasis on individual freedom as the goal of social life and in the Romantic conception of the social outsider. The Romantic imagination identifies spontaneously (as in Goethe's *Faust*) with the one who departs from convention or is condemned and cast out by those who enjoy the safety of unquestioned routines. This romanticization of the outcast became routinized in modern literature, and "Mrs. Grundy," the rigid upholder of proprieties in the face of life's need to escape them, became a proverbial object of scorn—

along with the proprieties themselves, whose importance to society came increasingly to be forgotten.

To the modern, post-Romantic imagination, therefore, the disposition to maintain social norms through stigma and shame seems abhorrent, a form of bad behavior rather than a cure for it. American culture has now firmly set itself against the old forms of social stigma, casting off its Puritan inheritance as something shameful—a novel cause for shame. The twentieth-century war on guilt has hastened this process. Thanks in part to the misreading and vulgarization of Freud by those who saw "repression" as an evil and "liberation" as the cure for it, and in part to the existentialist belief in "authenticity" and "good faith," guilt came to be seen as a negative force, a source of suffering with no compensating benefits.

Many theorists pressed toward this conclusion. Freud's pupil Wilhelm Reich, for example, attacked the "patriarchal family" as the source of sexual repression and of the deformation of the individual libido—as if sexual repression were an unquestionably bad thing. His *Function of the Orgasm* offered to liberate our sexual urges by providing them with a simple and morally neutral goal—not love or commitment or procreation or family, but a brief spasm of the flesh. Herbert Marcuse peddled the same wares in the language of Marxist humanism, while Sartre developed a whole theology of liberation, designed to portray conventional society, its norms and sanctions and conventions, as the source of all that is evil, all that prevents us from flowering in our freedom and enjoying the fruits of authentic choice. The greatest sin, for Sartre, was "bad faith"—obedience to an authority external to the self. Bad faith was the voice of the Other, and the principal enemy of human freedom is the right-thinking, law-abiding, and mutually vigilant community.

The attack on guilt involves a corresponding denial of

shame. If we are not to feel guilty about our sexual adventures, for example, then we cannot feel ashamed of them either. Moreover, any attempt to shame us, to hold us up to scorn or contempt for our seductions, orgies, and excesses, is an act of oppression, a negation of our fundamental rights. Henceforth, it was assumed, we are to regard the antics of our neighbors as entirely their own concern, no more to be criticized or ridiculed than the contents of their shopping carts as they reach the supermarket cash register. In the sexual sphere, as in the sphere of commodities, the only binding law is the law of the market.

The odd result of this movement to reject stigma, however, has been the introduction of stigma of another kind. "Judgmental" people find themselves condemned with a vehemence that would have gone down well in Salem. Those who live by the old morality end up paraded with abusive labels: if you deplore illegitimacy and the welfare dependency that often follows it, you show yourself to be "mean-spirited" and lacking in "compassion"; if you oppose the normalization of homosexuality, you are "homophobic"; if you believe in Western culture, you are an "elitist"—all labels that can damage a professional career. Stigma floats free in the anarchic world of individualist life-styles, ready to attach itself to anyone who stands up for self-restraint.

It is in this context that we should understand political correctness. The new kind of stigma creates a new kind of fear. Political correctness is not a morality in the traditional sense: it does not require you to change your life, to make sacrifices, or to live by an exacting code of conduct. It tells you to watch your language so as to avoid the only prevalent adverse judgment, which is judgment of the adverse judge. It tells you to speak inclusively of other cultures, other life-styles, other values: never take a disapproving stance or use words that might imply one. Hence the extreme volatility of the new speech codes. Any phrase or idiom that seems to imply judgment of another category or class of people can become, almost overnight, an object of stigma.

Unlike the old forms of stigma, however, whose function was to bind a community together and to seal each member into the common fate, this new form of stigma has precisely the opposite aim: to permit social fragmentation. The talk of "social inclusion" is a mask for the reverse. Political correctness does not seek to include the Other in "our" community but to accept his otherness and allow him to live outside. In effect, it is attempting to create a society of strangers, each pursuing his own gratification in his own freely chosen way, and none answerable for what he does to anyone but himself. Of course, there are limits: those activities that directly threaten life, limb, and property are still forbidden. But they are forbidden by law rather than morality. Moral codes, it is assumed, are ineffective and in any case of only "subjective" force. Insofar as we should have an attitude to the criminal, it too is one based on the attempt to "include" him, despite his error.

There is, however, one great exception to this attitude, and it goes to the heart of our moral nature. This exception is pedophilia. Britons have been up in arms for months over the case of Sarah Payne, an eight-year-old who was abducted, sexually abused, and murdered in June of this year. Sarah was, in her way, a perfect symbol of the old moral order—an innocent child of loving parents, brought up in a traditional family. The shattered faces of her mother and father on TV awoke in everyone not merely sympathy for their suffering but a confused awareness that they are martyrs. They represent the old moral code—and the world it once nurtured—in a society that no longer endorses it. They brought children into a world that no longer believes in childhood—that increasingly connives at the sexualization of children and allows them to set their own agendas, to adore their own idols, and to indulge their own simulacrum of desire. The pedophile is the one who has taken advantage of this situation, which no one has had the moral courage to prevent.

Of course, Sarah was murdered, and even in a shame-free culture, murder is a crime. But everyone knows that Sarah was murdered because she was the object of someone's lust, and that this lust is being normalized. Children in Britain, as in America, are compelled to attend "health education" classes in which they experiment with condoms; a British charity has just issued a guide to sex for children, entitled *Say Yes, Say No, Say Maybe* and explaining the various positions and excitements of intercourse; doctors prescribe contraceptive pills to underage girls and so make themselves accessories to what is officially a crime; the BBC broadcasts obscene and provocative films on television during hours when children are sure to be watching; children are represented in advertisements in alluring and provocative poses; and children's magazines are devoted to virtually no topic other than boyfriends and girlfriends.

Distress over the Sarah Payne case has led to an interesting development. The names of all convicted pedophiles in Britain are added to a register, so that schools, youth clubs, and others who might consider employing them can obtain notice in advance of the danger. Convicted pedophiles invariably leave the scenes of their crimes, knowing that their presence will not be tolerated there. And their attempts to start a new life are, in general, encouraged by the police. Since the Sarah Payne case, however, the Sunday *News of the World* has obtained a copy of the pedophile register and has printed the names, photographs, and addresses of those listed in it, together with details of their crimes. The police objected, seeing this as an invitation to criminal assault or worse. But for some weeks the paper continued its regular Sunday feature, profiting from the enormous public appetite for these details, now that the long-dormant desire to stigmatize has reawakened. Very soon, people named in its pages—some of them in error—were fleeing from their homes while vociferous crowds gathered outside to abuse, threaten, and assault them. One committed suicide; the police have relocated others at great public expense.

The case is additionally interesting in that the *News of the World* owes its readership to an undiluted diet of salacious stories of the kind retailed in school playgrounds, in which underwear and private parts feature prominently, often described in the language of schoolchildren. It also carries pictures of topless teenage girls who are, if not physically, at any rate mentally and morally children. The newspaper has tried to profit from the desire to stigmatize the thing that it also profits from by provoking.

The hysteria over pedophilia is indicative of a society that has come to the brink of self-destruction and stands there accusing the void. People reach for their old certainties: words like "pervert" and "perversion" suddenly seem right to them; they look round for the culprit with a view to shaming, humiliating, and ostracizing him. And they recognize the vastness of the evil that is around them and within them, an evil they only imperfectly confess to.

The confrontation between parents and pedophiles is a last-ditch battle on behalf of the old sexual morality, a final attempt to salvage the process whereby societies reproduce themselves not only physically but also morally. It is the most serious proof on offer that modern adults are still animated by the will to produce children who are objects of love and not fodder for appetite. Were political correctness to become the norm in this area too—as well it might, when the newly fashionable "rights of children" are extended to guarantee a right of sexual privacy, and when the British government succeeds in lowering the age of consent to homosexual sex to sixteen, an age when children are still compelled to go to school—then the "society of strangers" would at last be a reality. "Social inclusion" would mean social atomization, with no one caring a fig for others' behavior, provided only that he is not directly threatened by it, and with no one doing anything to ensure that the benefits and burdens of civilization are passed on.

Of course, we haven't reached that stage. Nevertheless, the permitted forms of stigmatization are dwindling. We know that some form of social control is necessary. Even in the prevailing climate of ignorance and denial, most people are able to draw from their sparse knowledge of history the conclusion that barbarism lies just below the surface, awaiting its opportunity to destroy. But people are afraid to judge their neighbors and hope that somehow the future of society will be taken care of, even though everyone is busy retreating from the arduous business of moral judgment.

As for the liberal intelligentsia, it seems to be unable to perceive the threat and blames every increase in social entropy on those who seek to contain it. Indeed, there seems to be a prevailing opinion among our elites that sexual mores are no longer a matter of public concern, that it is irrelevant to society that people should saturate their senses and their thoughts with violent, pornographic, or perverted images, and that, in any case, children will still be born, still grow up, still enjoy their years of innocence, still walk to school with their satchels on their backs and come home in the evening to *Alice in Wonderland* or at any rate Calvin and Hobbes. But this complacent belief is patently false: so bad are things in Britain that it is now a criminal offense to allow your child to walk unaccompanied on country lanes, and no parents in their right minds would allow their children out in the evenings even in a populous neighborhood—especially in a populous neighborhood.

The dwindling of stigma inevitably means that the task of social control is bequeathed to the state. The state has therefore become the guardian of social order. But this has happened at the very moment when the state sees no remedy for social ills besides "compassion," meaning the habit of subsidizing malefactors. The state no longer represents normal bourgeois society, its conventions and proprieties. Instead it has become subversive of those things, devoted to monopolizing all moral sanctions while at the same time voiding them of their force. Punishments are ever lighter, excuses ever more acceptable, and all opportunities to condemn or judge are smothered by a haze of political correctness.

To reproach your neighbor is to risk his goodwill; to uphold convention is to expose yourself to mockery from the liberated. And yet the good of society may require that ordinary people take these risks—risks that require courage, justice, and even a touch of humility if they are to be successfully managed. Modern literature has not often sung the heroism of the conventional conscience. But that heroism was sung beautifully by the Greeks, both in the choruses to the tragedies and in characters, such as Creon in the *Antigone* of Sophocles, who try to keep the ship of state afloat despite the passionate transgressions of its citizens. There is nothing that will serve us better than this old kind of heroism—the heroism of disapproval, whereby people risk condemnation for condemnation's sake. Stigma is not an act of aggression but a sign that we care about our neighbors' lives and actions. It expresses the consciousness of other people, the desire for their good opinion, and the impetus to uphold the social norms that make judgment possible. It is the outward expression of an inner orderliness— and a declaration of faith in human nature.

[2000]

BECOMING A FAMILY

I grew to immaturity in the sixties, at the moment famously, and ironically, described by Philip Larkin:

> Sexual intercourse began
> In nineteen sixty-three
> (Which was rather late for me)—
> Between the end of the Chatterley ban
> And the Beatles' first LP.

Young people of my generation had no time for Larkin's irony and simply dismissed traditional sexual morality as a clutter of meaningless taboos. The old culture endured among adults, especially those who had fought in the war and learned first-hand that societies depend on sacrifice. But the fidelity of our elders to the old mores merely caused our experiments to appear romantic and sophisticated in our own eyes, marks of a singular freedom of mind.

In truth, I didn't enjoy the spectacle of permissiveness and half suspected that the old morality was right. Nevertheless, I was not going to miss out on the available freedoms and felt entitled to my share of thrills. Like many of my generation, therefore, I was reluctant to marry and did so only when I discovered that my experiment in cohabitation had ceased to be an experiment and had become a commitment instead.

My wife-to-be had been brought up as a Roman Catholic

in provincial France. We had lived together through the antics of May 1968, which impressed both of us with the destructiveness and stupidity of people when guided by nothing more than a desire for liberation. Marriage was to bring an end to such childish things and to imbue our life with discipline.

In that spirit I attended the obligatory lessons with Father Napier of the Brompton Oratory in London, by way of preparing for the sacramental—and sacrificial—act. The Oratory retains the permitted vestiges of the Latin Mass and as a result has amplified its congregation of true believers with a reserve army of believers in belief, of which I was one. Next to the Italianate church, where its priests sing in their gorgeous robes and a four-part choir responds, stands an altogether humbler building, the residence of the Oratorians, whose order requires them not to fast and pray in seclusion but to go out and spread the word, obedient to the vision of St. Filippo Neri, their activist founder and high priest of the Counter-Reformation. Neri made the term "propaganda" part of the language, and the thing denoted by it part of life. But the home of his London followers, established in the last century by the great Cardinal Newman, has a dull, quotidian atmosphere; it is a place of quiet footsteps and mumbled greetings. Copperplate engravings of forgotten saints gather dust in corners, and the smell of institutional cooking wafts down corridors where nothing moves save a shuffling old priest, a fluttering curtain, or an aproned housemaid too old and stiff to brush the high cobwebs away.

In the room set aside for instruction, Father Napier rehearsed the tenets of the Catholic faith. I assented to them all: not one of them created the slightest intellectual difficulty, save the major premise of God's existence. But this too could be held in place, I surmised, by the structure that had been built upon it, and whose angles and junctures I knew from St.

Thomas Aquinas. A religion without orthodoxy is destined to be swept away by the first breath of doubt. When the doctrines are all in place, however, neatly interlocking, expressed and endorsed by ritual, then, I reasoned, none can be pried free from the edifice and exposed to questioning. The structure stands unshakably, even though built upon nothing. Seen in this way, religion is a work of art, and its values are aesthetic values: beauty, wholeness, symmetry, harmony.

Clearly, my attitude to the church whose rituals I was prepared to borrow was not ultimately the attitude of a believer. Hence when the marriage came under strain—which it very soon did, since our years of cohabitation had disenchanted our first love, while offering no second love in place of it—the religious chains proved to be made of paper.

Divorce appeared at the time in all the attractive colors of an easy option: a bid for freedom, a way to become what I truly and authentically was. Young people of my generation were told to seize their chances and to free themselves from guilt. Only too late do you discover that guilt is not a sickness to be overcome but a punishment to be lived through. The years following the end of my first marriage were filled with grief, and rightly so. Nobody should be allowed to get away scot-free from a life's commitment, and no one should treat lightly what is the most solemn vow. You can hope for forgiveness; but you have no right to expect it.

Nevertheless I learned from the experience. My guilt was a clear proof of the church's view of matrimony as an indissoluble tie. This doctrine, which at the time of my marriage had been for me merely an inert corollary to an abstract system of theology, now hit me in the face as a living truth about the human condition and a deep explanation of the ruined lives that I saw on every side, my own and my ex-wife's included.

For twenty years my efforts at romance would fizzle out,

quenched in the inward flow of lamentation. This process, if painful, was also purifying. It rid me of illusions and in particular of the illusion that sexual love is just an ordinary expression of our freedom. Often I recalled those quiet corridors of the Oratory and the foretaste they had offered of the penitential path beyond my marriage. A doctrine that permitted no other course save abstinence elevated marriage to a higher sphere, idealized it as a kind of redemption. What Father Napier had offered us through marriage was the very thing the Oratorians enjoyed in their place of dusty rituals: the transfiguration of everyday life.

When I met Sophie, six years ago, I knew how ridiculous it was for a man of fifty to propose marriage to a girl of twenty-two. But it was as though I had carried her portrait within me during twenty years of penitence and had suddenly happened upon her incarnation. We were introduced in the hunting field, constrained by the meticulous courtesies of which fox hunting is, in England, one of the few remaining preserves—the real reason our new rulers hate it. If romantic feelings arise in such a context, they come imbued with courtly hesitation. So it was with us, and it is part of what made us serious. Although impatient every Saturday for the moment when Sophie would appear, I was nonplussed in her presence, searching in vain for words. Then one day my horse fell, and she stopped to rescue me, so sacrificing the day's pleasure and giving proof that she cared. We began an old-fashioned courtship that lasted through many months of restraint.

Formality does not freeze emotion but heightens it. And emotions that take ritual shape lead of their own accord to that supreme ritual, which is marriage. By amplifying the distance between you, courtship intensifies the magnetic force when finally you join. Indeed, in our tradition—not necessarily the only or the best one, but the only one we have—marriage ought to be seen as the culmination of a process that begins in bashfulness and proceeds by stages to an intimacy both resisted and desired.

I was lucky: not everyone is given a second chance, certainly not a second chance like this one, in which sympathy sparked across the years made us welcome the barrier of age and then work to overcome it. When we awoke to what had happened, we knew that it was too late to think of any course but marriage, which had grown between us like a plant that had suddenly burst into flower.

Of course it matters what others think, and we, especially, needed their acceptance. The small-scale, furtive event in the registry office, hastily conducted like an illicit affair, would not have served our need. On the contrary, it would have seemed an admission that our spheres and years divided us and that we were making a dreadful mistake. We needed to make others complicit in our venture, to be bound together not just in private but also in the public eye. Ceremonies are redemptive. They raise private undertakings into public avowals and at the same time make the union of individuals into an emblem of the community's will to endure.

Modern society tends to construe marriage as a kind of contract. This tendency is familiar to us from the sordid divorces of tycoons and pop stars, and is made explicit in the "prenuptial agreement," under the terms of which an attractive woman sells her body at an inflated price, and a man secures his remaining assets from her future predations. Under such an agreement, marriage becomes a preparation for divorce, a contract between two people for the short-term exploitation of each other.

Surprisingly, it was the great Immanuel Kant who prepared the world for this view of things, describing marriage, in language of exemplary bleakness, as a "contract for the reciprocal use of the sexual organs." But then Kant didn't marry, and his heresy was soon corrected by Hegel, who did. According to Hegel, marriage is a "substantial tie." It begins in a contract—but it is a contract to transcend contract, by abolishing the separation between the parties.

Hegel's point can be put more simply. Marriage is surrounded by moral, legal, and religious prohibitions precisely because it is not a contract but a vow. Contracts have terms and come to an end when the terms are fulfilled or when the parties agree to renounce them. They bind us to the temporal world and have the transience of human appetite. Vows do not have terms, nor can they be legitimately broken. They are "forever"; and in making a vow you are placing yourself outside time and change, in a state of spiritual union which can be translated into actions in the here and now but also lies above and beyond the world of decaying things. That we can make vows is one part of the great miracle of human freedom; and when we cease to make them, we impoverish our lives by stripping them of lasting commitment.

Hence divorce does not end a real marriage, which will continue to bind those who have drifted away from it or who have tried to set its vows aside. For twenty years I was constantly aware of that other person, whom I no longer saw, but whose thoughts, feelings, and reproaches were addressed to me in my own inner voice. Sophie understood this and accepted it because she is the child of divorced parents, who took trouble never to quarrel in her presence and always to speak of each other with the respect due a fellow parent. Sophie was the living reminder of their vows and of the need to give due weight to them, and the marriage remained in a strange way untouchable, just because it was sacred in the eyes of a child.

Thanks to that great reservoir of fudge and compromise

that is the Anglican church, divorcés can now wed in church—not through a marriage ceremony but through a "service of dedication," designed to put a holy seal on the state's scrap of paper. Without presuming on, but nevertheless hoping for, forgiveness, you can petition the Almighty through this lesser ceremony and thereby summon the support and endorsement of your community. We married in a registry office and arranged the service of dedication for the next day, in Sophie's local church. We had rehearsed our vows and discovered as we spoke them that they were exactly what we felt. This promise to love, honor, and cherish till death us do part was precisely a recognition of our new state of unity.

Our feelings gained an added solemnity, now that all those on whose approval we depended were silently observing us. The words seemed to echo back from the unseen wall of sympathy in the church behind, and—far from announcing our bondage—they were a cry of liberation, the real liberation that comes through accepting a moral law. In my first marriage I had lost my freedom by wanting to hold on to it. In my second I regained it at the moment when I freely gave it away.

When we first met, I had just acquired the old farm where we now live. It is a truth universally acknowledged that a single man in possession of a house and thirty acres must be in want of a wife. But Sophie was as surprised by what happened as I was and entered my life almost on tiptoe, disturbing nothing and seeming to admire my bachelor ways at the same time as she gently and discreetly abolished them. Under her influence I became more outgoing and more relaxed, while never for a moment fearing that I might lose my carefully acquired routines and my armory of homegrown protections. There resulted from this an unusual division of roles: I do the cooking and the housework; she looks after the animals. We work at our desks in the day and ride out when we can. And whenever one of us crosses the house to peer at the other, it is always with a thrill of anticipation, like a child creeping up on its parent.

Sometimes we embark on a quarrel, but there is neither winner nor loser because we are one thing, not two, and any attack on the other becomes an attack on oneself. All the matters over which people like us are supposed to argue—money, freedom, visits, friends, hobbies, tastes, habits—become occasions for a deeper cooperation. What we have discovered through marriage is not the first love that induced it but the second love that follows, as the vow weaves life and life together. Western romanticism has fostered the illusion that first love is the truest love, and what need has first love of marriage? But an older and wiser tradition recognizes that the best of love comes after marriage, not before.

The birth of Sam did not change things. But it presented us with a problem that is particularly acute in Britain. The state now forces us to send our children to school while ensuring that nothing much in the way of education occurs there. What passes for education in many British schools is really a process of demoralization, in which children are taken from their parents and surrendered to their peers. Today significant numbers of young Britons leave school unable to read or do mental arithmetic. Useless old subjects like Latin, Greek, and higher mathematics have disappeared, and English grammar, with its oppressive rules and useless complexities, has been pushed aside as "elitist." As for manners, these have declined to such an extent that shops near London schools regularly close their doors to children while older people seek refuge in another car when children board a train.

Instead of preparing children for adult life, our system of education ensures that they remain children, with all of childhood's self-centered incompetence but none of its redeeming innocence and shame. The state's attempt to sexualize children—encouraging members of the younger generation to master all the relevant positions by the age of fourteen, and making homosexuality a central part of their curriculum—doesn't help matters. Sex, pupils learn, is just an extension of childhood—another realm of play, in which all is permitted that could lead to enjoyment, and in which only the serious, the lasting, and the loving are dangerous.

The sixties' ideology, which caused such havoc in my own personal life, and the evil effects of which it took me twenty years to overcome, is now an obligatory basis of schooling, enforced from the tenderest age, and with complete disregard for the personal happiness and long-term hopes of the pupils. What I escaped only with the greatest difficulty and by the skin of my teeth is now being imposed as a general destiny. Surely the first of my duties toward Sam is to ensure that he does not fall into the clutches of the people who want to do this to him.

The new curriculum, which has both the aim and the effect of cutting off children from their parents, making them unlovable to adults and the exclusive property of the state, springs from the minds of people who are themselves, for the most part, childless. It would be better, it seemed to us, for Sam to be sent down a coal mine, there to encounter the real world of adults, than to go through the complete course in demoralization that our rulers require. Even the private schools must follow the National Curriculum, which has been carefully devised to remove all the knowledge that Sophie and I value and to substitute the "life skills" needed in an urban slum.

The only solution that has occurred to us so far is to educate Sam ourselves for as long as time, energy, and knowledge permit and then to send him to the Lycée Français in London, on the understanding that the French have been slightly less contemptuous toward their national culture than we have been. As to what Sam's curriculum should be, common sense directs us down the old and beaten path. And we shall start him off with Grimm, Andersen, and Lewis Carroll, since their brand of children's literature does not merely enlarge the imagination: it also educates the moral sense.

While pondering this matter, however, I was invited by a national newspaper to describe what we intended for Sam—a sign that many people share our concerns. Naturally, I assured the readers, if John Stuart Mill could read Greek at six, why not Sam? And maybe Sam's first public utterance could match that of the four-year-old Macaulay, deflecting the meddlesome attentions of a toddler-coddler, after he had hurt himself, with the words: "I thank you, Madam, the agony is abated." Sam would be kept away from pop music and television but would study the viola as a salutary form of self-abasement. He would be introduced to horses and fox hunting, so as to learn both to care for animals and to do so unsentimentally. He would be taught the virtues—courage, justice, prudence, and temperance—in their Christian version, as forms of faith, hope, and charity. And although Sam would probably not enjoy his childhood, I wrote, he would emerge from it as someone agreeable to others, whether or not happy in himself.

The article precipitated a storm of abuse from experts in child-rearing, educational gurus, feminists, and assorted believers in progress—all manifestly products of an education system that identifies irony as an elitist crime and has therefore extinguished the ability to understand it. For several weeks we lived in dread of the social workers. If we could not answer their inquiries, we feared, Sam would be put into foster care, denied all access to his parents, and given a normal diet of pop, television, and takeout.

The experts who greeted our educational plans with such

outrage were, after all, the voice of our modern culture—the very same culture that has shaped the educational system and set up the state in opposition to the family. It is only since becoming part of a family that I have fully gauged the depth and seriousness of this opposition. The family has become a subversive institution—almost an underground conspiracy—at war with the state and the state-sponsored culture.

Hence the official curriculum has rigorously excluded the family. Mothers appear from time to time in schoolbooks, but they are conspicuously single. Fathers are never mentioned—indeed, they have become unmentionable, as trousers were to our Victorian ancestors. The state-imposed sex education is designed to sever the link between sex and the family by showing the family to be merely an "option." Sex education will ensure that the next generation will not form families, since it will have destroyed in its pupils everything that leads one sex to idealize the other and so to channel erotic feelings into marriage.

But Sophie and I have no doubt that it is the family, not the state, that fulfills us. Hence we have decided to follow our own instincts and observations, and to bring up our children as we believe to be right. We are members of a growing class of criminals who have declared war on the state-sponsored culture and are prepared to challenge it.

This official culture is founded on the premise that the human material is infinitely plastic and can be molded by the state into any shape required. This is one of the first of the official doctrines that you learn, as a parent, to doubt. We compared Sam with other boys and could not help remarking how similar they are in one fundamental respect: which is, that they all want to be men. Moreover, they all associate manliness with action, with the use of tools, with the making of something out of nothing, and with power and the machines that produce it. Sam has shown little concern for language, has entirely neglected not only the viola but also the guitar and the piano, and has confined his musical experiments to turning on the rhythm machine of my electronic keyboard whenever he sees me working.

His principal interest is building. He spends his days with the men who are working on our extension—handing out trowels, heaving buckets, mixing his own version of cement and occasionally using it to make plaster casts of living chickens. Although he is unlikely to emulate either Mill or Macaulay, his eager, cooperative nature, his determination to be useful, and his narrow but real curiosity about the world of masculine labor has endeared him to many hearts.

The official doctrine attributes such tendencies to culture: change the toys, the role models, and the contexts, the experts say, and boys will dress up, play with dolls, coddle animals, and make little interiors where they can be snug as a bug in a rug. But there seems to be a paucity of supporting evidence for such a view. Science, common sense, and recorded history all point to the conclusion that sex is a constant, which influences what can be achieved and what can be desired. Rather than work against it, we should work with it, to use its vast and unconscious power to drive our civilizing purpose.

The birth of our baby girl Lucy again awoke our curiosity in this respect, and while we of course intend to bring her up in the same improving regime that we proposed for Sam, we are fairly sure that she will not be seen, twelve months hence, with a trowel in her hand. Lucy's first smile was enough to convince us of this. Whereas Sam grinned broadly and mischievously, and then reached out to tear down the toy horse that hung above his crib, Lucy offered a serene, observing twinkle. Friends and neighbors all confirm the view that little girls are interested in people, in words, in the intimate togetherness of home, and that tools and machines fail to awaken their sympathies.

Why should people resist the obvious when it comes to sexual roles? The answer, I believe, goes to the heart of our modern anxieties. In the world described by Jane Austen, men and women enjoyed separate spheres of action, the first public, the second private, the first involving influence without intimacy, the second an intimacy that was also a form of far-reaching, though publicly hidden, influence. Dress, manners, education, recreation, and language all reinforced this division, with marriage as the great life-choice in which it culminated and whose purpose it was. Because there is no going back to Jane Austen's world, we take refuge in the belief that every aspect of it reflects some arbitrary cultural imperative, with nothing due to permanent human nature. By extending cultural relativism even into those spheres where it is not culture but nature that determines what we do, we deceive ourselves into accepting—but with anxiety—a situation so novel that our ancestors never even thought to guard against it: the situation in which men and women are exchangeable in all their social roles and all their spheres of action.

It seems to me, however, that we do our children a disservice if we fail to acknowledge that their sexual nature sets them from the beginning on different paths. We should learn not to deny sex but to idealize it—to set before our children an image of the good man and the good woman, and to teach them to imitate what can be loved and admired. Even without the old division of roles, we can envisage alternative forms of role-playing that serve a comparable function—that rescue sex from animal appetite and make it the foundation of a lasting commitment.

Children, in their innocence, have an inkling of this. Sam

with his trowel is idealizing himself; just as Lucy will idealize herself as she reads stories to her dolls and tends their fictitious ailments. Idealization is natural to human beings; for it is the process whereby they try to make themselves lovable and to live in the only security that our life provides. In our marriage vows, Sophie and I were making the same attempt. We knew the fickle lot of the human animal; we knew that married life would be fraught with temptations and frustrations. But we knew also that those things are not the only reality. We become fully human when we aim to be more than human; it is by living in the light of an ideal that we live with our imperfections. That is the deep reason why a vow can never be reduced to a contract: the vow is a pledge to the ideal light in you; a contract is signed by your self-interested shadow.

You do no service to a child by preparing him for the lower life—the life of the state-produced animal. Happiness comes through ideals, and it is only by idealizing each other that people can really fall in love. Such is the lesson that Sophie and I draw from our own experience, and we are surely not unique in this but normal human beings. The strange superstition has arisen in the Western world that we can start all over again, remaking human nature, human society, and the possibilities of happiness, as though the knowledge and experience of our ancestors were now entirely irrelevant. But on what fund of knowledge are we to draw when framing our alternative? The utopias have proved to be illusions, and the most evident result of our "liberation" from traditional constraints has been widespread discontent with the human condition.

It seems to me, therefore, that you should prepare your children to be happy in the way that you are happy. Treat them exactly as you would if your own ideals were generally shared. One day they will find, as we have found, the partner who makes it all worthwhile. Knowing this, we can reapply ourselves to the education of Sam and Lucy, systematically depriving them, day after day, of the things our rulers recommend.

[2001]

A NOTE ON THE CONTRIBUTORS

Theodore Dalrymple is a physician who regularly sees patients in an English prison. He is a contributing editor of *City Journal*, a columnist for the *London Spectator*, and a frequent contributor to the *Daily Telegraph*. His latest book is *Life at the Bottom: The Worldview That Makes the Underclass*, a collection of his *City Journal* stories.

Kay S. Hymowitz, a contributing editor of *City Journal*, is the author of *Ready or Not: Why Treating Children as Small Adults Endangers Their Future and Ours*. She has written for the *Wall Street Journal*, *The New Republic*, and the *New York Times*.

Myron Magnet, editor of *City Journal*, is the author of *The Dream and the Nightmare: The Sixties' Legacy to the Underclass*, which George W. Bush names as the book that has influenced him most, after the Bible. He is also the editor of *The Millennial City* and *What Makes Charity Work?*

Roger Scruton is a writer and philosopher living in England. He is a contributing editor of *City Journal* and the author of *Sexual Desire: A Moral Philosophy of the Erotic* and *An Intelligent Person's Guide to Modern Culture*. His most recent book is *England: an Elegy*.

Wendy Shalit is a contributing editor of *City Journal* and the author of *A Return to Modesty: Discovering the Lost Virtue*.

Harry Stein is a contributing editor of *City Journal*. A journalist and novelist, he is most recently the author of *How I Accidentally Joined the Vast Right-Wing Conspiracy: (And Found Inner Peace)*.

Barbara Dafoe Whitehead is the author of *The Divorce Culture: Rethinking Our Commitments to Marriage and Family* and is a regular contributor to *The Atlantic Monthly*.

INDEX